GOD IS IN THE SMALL STUFF

for Your Marriage

GOD IS IN THE SMALL STUFF

for Your Marriage

Bruce & Stan

PROMISE PRESS

An Imprint of Barbour Publishing

Unless otherwise noted, Scripture is taken from the HOLY BIBLE: New International Version®. NIV®. Copyright © 1973, 1978, 1984 by International Bible Society. Used by permission of Zondervan Plublishing House.

Scripture quotations marked NLT are taken from the *Holy Bible,* New Living Translation, copyright 1996. Used by permission of Tyndale House Publishers, Inc., Wheaton, Illinois 60189, USA. All rights reserved.

Published by Promise Press, an imprint of Barbour Publishing, Inc., P.O. Box 719, Uhrichsville, Ohio 44683, http://www.barbourbooks.com

Member of the
Evangelical Christian
Publishers Association

Printed in the United States of America.

CONTENTS

INTRODUCTION

LOVE AND ROMANCE

Thinking of You 13

Dating Doesn't Stop with the Wedding. 19

Loving and Liking 25

Finding Occasions to Celebrate 29

Physical Intimacy 35

COMMUNICATION

Making Time for Your Spouse 39

Showing Love Says Love 43

Ten Ways to Sabotage Your Marriage 47

Speaking a Language Your Spouse Understands 51

A Good Kind of Surprise 57

SPIRITUAL GROWTH

Let God Come between You. 61

Prayer Holds You Together 65

Reading the Marriage Manual 69
Church Differences. 75
God Knows What Your Marriage Needs. 79

PERSONAL GROWTH
Space Planning: Making Room to Grow. 83
Opposites Attract 87
Lessons from Nature. 91
The Joy of Becoming 97
When Your Growth Spurts Are out of Sync 101

CHILDREN
When and How Many 105
Parenting 101 111
The Care and Coaching of Teenagers 115
Leave Your Kids Before They Leave You. 119
No Kids? Know Kids! 123

FAMILY AND FRIENDS
You Married an Entire Family. 127
Out with the In-Laws. 133
The Old Gang and the Old Hangouts 137

Love Thy Neighbor 141
Compatibility Times Two 147

FINANCES

Fiscal Intimacy 151
Yours, Mine, and Ours 155
Paper or Plastic? 159
Who's in Charge? 163

WORK

Who Cooks the Bacon If Both Bring It Home? . . . 167
Time Pressure and Fatigue 171
Working Together: You Aren't the Boss of Me! . . . 177
Keeping Your Affections at Home
    (Where They Belong) 183

RECREATION

Vacations Are Supposed to Be a Waste of Time . . . 189
Exercise. . .Even If It Kills You 195
You Can't Afford Another Fad 199
The Best Things in Life Are Free 205

FOR WIVES ONLY

The Male Ego: Handle with Care. 209

The Dreaded "S" Word

(and we don't mean "sex") 213

The Other Dreaded "S" Word

(this time we do mean what you think) 219

FOR HUSBANDS ONLY

Where Sex Begins 223

Avert Your Glance 227

The True Meaning of Love. 233

GROWING OLDER TOGETHER

Redecorate Your Lives. 237

Now Your Nest Is Empty—Now It's Not! 241

Don't Let Your Golden Years Turn Brown. 247

Your Marriage Is Your Greatest Legacy. 251

INTRODUCTION

A popular book suggests that you don't worry about the small stuff. We agree, but we take exception to any idea that the small stuff isn't important. In fact, we want to encourage you to closely examine and cherish the seemingly everyday, ordinary circumstances of your life. Why? Because God is in the details of your life.

Marriage has been called a sacred treasure. Others see it as nothing more than a social contract. We happen to believe the first description for one very simple reason: Marriage is God's idea. In the beginning God created the heavens and the earth and people. Adam and Eve were the first couple, designed to enjoy each other and glorify God. Realizing that God had done this, the author of Genesis exclaimed:

> *This explains why a man leaves his father and mother and is joined to his wife, and the two are united into one.*
>
> —GENESIS 2:24

A lot has changed since those days, but marriage is still the process that unites a husband and wife. Notice we said process. Much more than a simple "I do" and a legal pronouncement, marriage is a living, breathing, ongoing relationship that changes two people for the better and affects all those around them.

God isn't just interested in your marriage ceremony, even though you are wise to include Him. And He isn't there only when you call upon Him in a time of need, although He promises to answer. God is involved in every detail of your lives, for your benefit and for the good of your marriage.

That's why we have titled this book, *God Is in the Small Stuff for Your Marriage*. It's true! He's there for you every step of the way: when you say, "I do," when you find great happiness, when you experience difficult times, when your children arrive, and when you grow old together. No matter what you do, no matter where you go, God is there.

> *I can never escape from your spirit!*
> *I can never get away from your presence!*
> *If I go up to heaven, you are there;*

if I go down to the place of the dead, you are there.
If I ride the wings of the morning,
if I dwell by the farthest oceans,
even there your hand will guide me,
and your strength will support me.

—PSALM 139:7–10

This book contains fifty-two essays that reflect on God's involvement in the circumstances of your marriage. Maybe you've been married for a while. Perhaps you are a newlywed, or marriage may be in your future. Your marriage may be the best it's ever been or "on the rocks." Whatever your situation, we want you to know that God cares about the small stuff for your marriage.

Oswald Chambers wrote: "We can all see God in exceptional things, but it requires the growth of spiritual discipline to see God in every detail." May this book help you and your spouse as you grow together spiritually.

Bruce & Stan

I t only takes a moment each day
to secure love for a lifetime.

Bruce & Stan

LOVE AND ROMANCE

ONE

THINKING
OF YOU

There is an old joke about a husband and wife who visit a marriage counselor on their twenty-fifth wedding anniversary. When asked the reason for their visit, the wife complains: "In twenty-five years of marriage, my husband has never said 'I love you' to me." The husband retorts: "I said 'I love you' at the wedding ceremony, and that stays in effect until I revoke it." This joke evokes some laughter from husbands and wives, but it is mostly nervous laughter (because there is a lot of painful truth in this little joke).

One of the quickest ways to choke the romance out of marriage is to take each other for granted. Don't let that happen. Keep the romance in your marriage alive by letting your spouse know that you are so much in love that you can't stop thinking about him or her. Find ways to remind your spouse that he or she occupies your thoughts even though your schedules keep you separated most of the day.

During the phases of dating, courtship, and engagement, you and your spouse probably spent most of your day thinking about each other. And you probably let each other know it, too. Phone calls, notes, and endless conversations were evidence that you were always thinking of each other. But with marriage comes familiarity, and while familiarity doesn't always breed contempt (with apologies to Ben Franklin or whoever made that famous quote), familiarity does often bring routine. And in the routine of life we often forget to let our spouse know that he or she remains a priority in our lives—and in our thoughts throughout the day.

Take a lesson from God Himself. He knew human nature. And He knew that Moses and the Israelites could quickly forget about God in the midst of their daily routines even though He had rescued them from slavery in Egypt. (Your spouse forgetting your anniversary seems fairly innocuous compared to the Israelites forgetting that God saved them from the plagues of boils, locusts, frogs, and death that He wreaked on Pharaoh.) God gave specific instructions to Moses to ensure that the Israelites kept thinking about Him throughout the day:

> *And you must love the LORD your God with all*
> *your heart, all your soul, and all your strength.*
> *And you must commit yourselves wholeheartedly*
> *to these commands I am giving you today.*
> *Repeat them again and again to your children.*
> *Talk about them when you are at home and*
> *when you are away on a journey, when you are*
> *lying down and when you are getting up again.*
> *Tie them to your hands as a reminder, and wear*
> *them on your forehead. Write them on the door-*
> *posts of your house and on your gates.*
>
> DEUTERONOMY 6:5–9

With these kinds of constant reminders, God would not be forgotten or ignored in the routine of the day. Instead, He became a part of the routine.

Your spouse should be an integral part of your day. We aren't suggesting that you put your spouse in first place in the priorities of your life. That place belongs to God. But your spouse should be in second place. And you should take extra effort to make sure that your spouse knows that you are thinking of him or her throughout the day. It shouldn't overload your creativity circuitry to come up with a few ways to communicate this fact. How about going back to those calls, notes, and conversations that you used in the past? Place a "thinking of you" note in a desk drawer, on the car dashboard, or in a briefcase. Or make a call during the afternoon for no other reason than to say, "I love you."

Don't let the routine of daily living suppress your expressions of love for your spouse. Instead, make sure that your spouse knows that he or she has a place of priority in your thoughts throughout the day.

. . .IN THE SMALL STUFF

- Your spouse shouldn't have to think back to your wedding ceremony to remember the last time you said, "I love you."

- You have a lot of things on your mind. Make sure your spouse knows that he or she is one of them.

- Thinking fondly of your spouse might make you feel better, but it won't do anything for your spouse unless you express your fondness.

- Replace the coffee break with a call to your spouse. Instead of caffeine, let romance be your central nervous system's stimulant.

If couples would put
half the effort into marriage
that they put into courtship,
they would be surprised
how things would brighten up.

Billy Graham

TWO

DATING DOESN'T STOP
WITH THE WEDDING

Remember that combination of nervousness and excitement you felt when you first started dating your spouse? Of course, he or she wasn't your spouse then. The first time you went out, you hardly knew each other. But isn't that why you dated? You wanted to get to know him. You wanted to find out what she was like—and what she liked.

Your dates were fun. You looked forward to a special

evening or day, a time you both had set aside so you could spend time together and enjoy each other's company. Eventually, your dating experience convinced you that this was the person you wanted to live with the rest of your life. Then you got married. And the dating stopped.

What a shame.

If dating was so much fun and gave you the opportunity to really get to know your future spouse, why did you stop? Now that you're married, are you no longer interested in having fun? Do you know everything about your spouse that you could ever need or want to know?

Maybe you are at the point where being married is more work than fun. You may be bored with your spouse, and you're looking for some excitement. Look no further. Your spouse still has those qualities that attracted you in the first place, and now there's even more. That's right, whether you realize it or not, your marriage partner has grown in positive ways that you have yet to uncover. All you have to do is make a decision to start dating again, and you will find the wonderful person you married is better and more interesting than ever.

By its very definition, a date is "an appointment to engage in some sort of social activity." So treat it that way. When you were wooing your honey, you didn't just show up on her doorstep unannounced and say, "I'm here, let's go out." You didn't tell your knight in shining armor, "I don't feel like going out. I have a headache."

No, you planned ahead, you came up with a creative idea for your date, you called her up and asked her out. You eagerly anticipated the date, put it on your calendar, and counted the days.

Do the same thing now. Think of a special activity or place, call her up (or call him up), and make a date. As busy as you both are, you need to make an appointment. Then, when the time for the date arrives, get ready. Just like you made yourself look and smell as good as you could when you were dating, look good for your spouse now. One of the keys to a healthy marriage is continuing to attract your husband or wife.

When you are actually on the date, show interest in the other person. Ask questions. You don't know everything about your mate—and besides, he's growing in ways you haven't noticed. She's changing as a person, and you haven't taken the time to discover how. Dating will do wonders for your marriage. It may even revive your relationship.

. . .IN THE SMALL STUFF

- Make dating a habit. Do it once a month at the very least.

- Be creative on your dates, and don't think you have to spend a lot of money.

- Recover the lost art of opening doors and pulling out chairs for your wife.

- Tell your husband how handsome he looks, even if he does have less hair and more weight now than when you first met him.

- Find another couple who shares your passion for dating, and then agree to take care of their kids if they will take care of yours when you date.

- Every once in a while, give your date a gift.

- For a real change of pace, end your date in a hotel room.

- It doesn't matter how long you've been married. Always treat your date with respect.

We don't naturally grow together
and love each other more.
We tend to grow apart, to grow distant.
So we have to work hard at marriage.
It's the most fun work in the world,
but it's still work.

Anne Ortlund

THREE

LOVING
AND LIKING

T here is a significant differ-
ence between *liking* and *loving*. Liking is usually a precedent to
loving, but that doesn't mean that the liking in your relationship becomes superfluous when you are married. Both liking
and loving are essential ingredients to a strong marriage.

Love brings a sense of commitment that belongs in
marriage. After all, isn't that what we mean to convey when
we say our vows to each other at the wedding ceremony?

Certainly we intend to express a pledge of commitment when we utter words like "till death do us part." That promise is at the core of what "love" means. When we say, "I love you," we are saying, in effect, "I am committed to you no matter what."

Perhaps the most famous verse in the Bible is John 3:16, which reads:

> *For God so loved the world that he gave his only Son, so that everyone who believes in him will not perish but have eternal life.*

The true meaning of that verse is illustrated when you define love as commitment:

> *For God was so committed to the world that He gave his only Son. . . .*

But a marriage held together by commitment alone can result in loneliness for both the husband and wife. There needs to be *liking* in the marriage. The husband and wife need to be each other's best friend. They need to enjoy the company of each other and desire to spend time with each other more than with anyone else.

Make sure your marriage is filled with both loving and liking. And the next time your spouse asks, "I know you *love* me, but do you *like* me?" you won't have to fumble for an answer. You can confidently state:

"One of the reasons I *love* you so much is because I *like* you so much!"

. . .In the Small Stuff

- Loving your spouse provides the stability in your marriage. Liking your spouse provides the fun.

- Marriage is a loving relationship between best friends.

- "I love you" should be a frequently repeated phrase in your marriage.

- Every once in a while, tell people that you are in love with your best friend. (It will give them something to gossip about.)

Marriage is the alliance of two people,
one of whom never remembers birthdays
and the other never forgets them.

Ogden Nash

FOUR

FINDING OCCASIONS TO CELEBRATE

A celebration can take many forms. It can be a party with family and friends to honor a birthday. A celebration can be rather formal, like a program to commemorate a notable achievement. Or it can be a quiet dinner in your favorite restaurant to celebrate your anniversary.

Like everything else in your marriage, successful celebrations take planning and work. They don't just happen. On the other hand, the important events you intend to celebrate (like birthdays and anniversaries) tend to happen whether you're ready or not. They occur even when you can't remember them, which usually leads to great embarrassment.

Here's our remedy for remembering key events in your married life that happen regularly: Put them in your calendar (or Day-Timer or Palm Pilot or whatever you use). We even suggest that you go one step further and log in a reminder ahead of time—one month ahead for birthdays and three months ahead for anniversaries. That way you'll have the time to make those dinner or hotel reservations at really nice places, rather than settling for last-minute choices like Burger King or the Motel 6 on the Interstate.

Birthdays and anniversaries may be the most obvious reasons to celebrate, but they are not the only ones. We strongly recommend that you find other occasions to celebrate each other and your marriage. In fact, we'd like to go as far as to suggest that you find at least one occasion each month.

A monthly schedule of celebrations coincides nicely with our recommendation to date your spouse once a month. (It's okay to combine your celebrations with your dates, unless you're planning to celebrate with forty other people.) It also shows tremendous respect for your husband or wife and your marriage.

Here are a few ideas:

- You can celebrate achievement: "Honey, you lost those ten pounds you wanted to lose, you look great, so let's go celebrate by buying you some new clothes."

- You can celebrate a promotion: "I knew you could do it, so I've made reservations at the Mother Lode Bed & Breakfast, which we can easily afford with the raise you're getting."

- You can celebrate an accomplishment: "Both kids are in school, so let's go to lunch on Fridays."

And then there are those built-in times of celebration, such as Valentine's Day, Mother's Day, Father's Day, and Veteran's Day. (Hey, you're veterans. . .marriage veterans.) Yeah, the whole world may be having dinner on Valentine's Day, but this is not the time to be a non-conformist. A box of chocolates and a gift certificate to Pic n' Save is no substitute for a dozen roses and a romantic dinner at Chez Pricey.

Finally, try celebrating your marriage on a day separate from your wedding anniversary. Call it your Marriage Anniversary. Here's what you do. Once a year—say, six months from your wedding anniversary—take stock of your married life. Celebrate the blessings, not the battles; focus on the fun you have, not the frustrations you experience. Talk together over dinner and recognize how God has provided for you in every detail of your marriage. See Him in the small stuff of your blessed union of souls, which goes even deeper than your love, right to your very spirit.

Hey, you never know. If this Marriage Anniversary idea takes hold, maybe we can design some cards for the occasion. If that happens, you will be the first to know!

. . .IN THE SMALL STUFF

- There's nothing wrong with asking people (other than your wife or husband) to help you remember special occasions.

- Generally speaking, a woman would rather have dinner and talk than go to a game and cheer.

- Generally speaking, men prefer an evening where conversation isn't the main feature.

- Don't get stuck in a rut. Plan a variety of celebrations throughout the year.

Marriage is popular because
it combines the maximum of temptation
with the maximum of opportunity.

George Bernard Shaw

FIVE

PHYSICAL
INTIMACY

What do you suppose God thinks marriage should be like? After all, He invented it with Adam and Eve in the Garden of Eden (in what was the first arranged marriage). Do you think God considers that marriage should be the platonic union of a male and female for the primary purpose of maintaining an orderly society (with the occasional exception for essential procreation)? We think not.

God wants your marriage to be physically pleasurable

for both you and your spouse. Absolutely, positively, and without a doubt, God wants you to find sensual enjoyment with your spouse. How can we be so convinced of this divine intention? Well, first of all, we are guys, so what do you expect us to say? But our proof is in the fact that God specifically designed the male and female bodies. He came up with the whole idea of sex, and He gave to each gender the equipment, tools, and parts that are compatibly pleasurable for the other.

God's design for physical intimacy is always within the context of marriage. Oh, the equipment, tools, and parts still work outside of marriage, but the emotional, mental, and spiritual elements of a lifelong commitment are missing when that happens. And those are the very elements that add meaning, significance, and enjoyment to physical intimacy.

God intended for you to have an intimate relationship with your spouse. Intimacy implies privacy and exclusivity. The deep bond of intimacy that God designed for marriage requires that the physical expressions of affection are shared exclusively between spouses. Within that sacred context, you are doing exactly what God intended for you when you enjoy physical pleasures with your spouse.

- There is a time and a place for love: any time and any place.

- Man is like a gas stove, quickly turned on and quickly turned off after ignition.

- Woman is like an electric stove, slow to glow, then ready to go, then slow to glimmer and ever more gradually dimmer.

- Physical intimacy between a husband and wife is a lot like fireworks: The roman candles and skyrockets don't have to explode simultaneously, so long as they aren't always both duds.

- Physical intimacy can include laughing, and it can include pointing. But it should never permit laughing and pointing at the same thing.

What we lack is not time,
but heart.

Henri Boulard

COMMUNICATION

SIX

MAKING TIME
FOR YOUR SPOUSE

There really is no such thing as "making" time. Time is already made, already measured out in equal doses to everyone. You can't create any more time than you have.

What you can do is redistribute your time so that you spend less of it on the things that don't matter as much, and more on the things that do. The problem we all face is that time is like water in a river: It flows to the place of least resistance. For you that could be work or television or some kind of recreation. Now, work and television and recreation are fine, but if you don't resist, a lot of your "extra" time will flow there, taking time away from really important stuff, like your marriage.

You see, marriage doesn't cry out for time. It's just there, always a part of you. On the other hand, your work is full of deadlines and projects and meetings that clamor for your time. Television is an escape from reality, and recreation is just so much fun. Yeah, marriage has its rewards, but it takes a lot of work.

Bingo. Because marriage takes work, it takes time—time to talk things out, to really listen to your spouse, to reveal your expectations and share your dreams. So how do you get this extra time? By "damming up" those other areas, which means you set time boundaries around them and direct more time to your marriage. That way the time you spend working, watching, and playing won't flood your marriage.

When you purposefully limit the time you spend doing things outside your marriage—work, for example—you aren't necessarily decreasing your chances of success. In fact, your time discipline may actually help you succeed, because you will make more efficient use of your time.

People will respect you for budgeting your schedule so you have enough time for your marriage. And no one will respect you more than your spouse.

. . .IN THE SMALL STUFF

- Sit down with your spouse regularly and compare calendars. Make sure you both are happy with the time you are giving to each other.

- Time flies by, but you can direct the direction it flies.

- No one has more time than you.

- No one has less time than you.

- When it comes to the river of time, we are all in the same boat.

They do not love
who do not show their love.

William Shakespeare

SEVEN

SHOWING LOVE
SAYS LOVE

It's easy to say: "I love you." (The expression is only three words long, and they are all short.) Unfortunately, the expression is over used. Sure, you say you love your spouse, but you also say you love mint-chip ice cream. We are at the point where the word "love" only takes on real meaning when you put action behind it.

We have no doubt that your spouse enjoys hearing your declarations of love. But we also have no doubt that your spouse would enjoy (perhaps even more) the different ways you might show your love instead of just saying it. Actions do speak louder than words, whether the actions are practical or romantical (we know that's not a word, but we're being poetic).

For husbands, this might mean:
- Practical: Doing household chores without being reminded.
- Romantical: Taking your wife out for dinner at a nice restaurant (which we define as a place where you don't take your meal to the table on a plastic tray).

For wives, this might mean:
- Practical: Washing your husband's car because you know he will never get around to doing it.
- Romantical: Wearing the negligée he bought you from Victoria's Secret (even though it is uncomfortable and not as cozy as the flannel nightgown you prefer to wear).

Show love at least as often as you speak of love. If you

can get out of bed at 11 P.M. and drive to the store for a quart of that mint-chip ice cream you love so much, we're sure that you can go to a little extra effort for that spouse you love so much.

. . .IN THE SMALL STUFF

- Talk is cheap. Don't let your actions be described the same way.

- If you were mute and couldn't speak, how would you tell your spouse of your love? Try it for a while. Your spouse will appreciate the creativity (and perhaps the silence).

- Your words of love are much more believable if your actions are consistent with them.

- It might take longer to show "I love you" than to say "I love you," but the memory lasts longer, too.

Lord, when we are wrong,
make us willing to change,
and when we are right,
make us easy to live with.

Peter Marshall

EIGHT

TEN WAYS TO SABOTAGE YOUR MARRIAGE

If your marriage is troubling you—or worse, in trouble—it's probably not because of any one big thing. It's probably a bunch of small stuff that you have allowed to go on in your life. These are those proverbial "irreconcilable differences" you always read about, the ones that happen to other couples but never to you.

Like a piece of sand in an oyster, these small irritations accumulate until they're much bigger. Except in this case, you don't end up with a beautiful pearl, but something much less attractive. Just because this stuff happens doesn't mean you're an irresponsible spouse. Only when you let the negative small stuff go on unchecked do problems develop. So in the interest of helping you identify some of these grains of sand, here are ten ways to sabotage your marriage:

1. Be a flirt.
2. Undermine your spouse in public.
3. Use negative body language when your spouse is talking to you.
4. Fail to truly communicate on a daily basis.
5. Stop caring about your appearance.
6. Have children in order to bring your marriage together.
7. Men: Enjoy playing golf (or whatever takes your time) more than you enjoy your wife.
8. Women: Spend more time with your friends (or whatever takes your time) than you spend with your husband.
9. Find your self-esteem outside the marriage.
10. Conceal your expectations.

Do a quick check and see how many of these are true for you now. Then do your best to change your direction before your abrasive behavior begins to sabotage your marriage. Work to create an "oyster marriage," one that turns life's small irritations into beautiful and precious "pearls."

. . .IN THE SMALL STUFF

- Accept this undeniable truth: All husbands and wives are going to have differences.

- Don't let little differences build up until they become big problems.

- See your differences as endearing rather than annoying.

- Compliment your spouse in front of other people.

- Talk in glowing terms about your spouse when he or she isn't around.

I wouldn't object to
my wife having the last word—
if only she'd get to it.

Henny Youngman

NINE

SPEAKING A LANGUAGE
YOUR SPOUSE UNDERSTANDS

Communication problems are obstacles that many marriages can't hurdle. Both the husband and wife can be considerate and well-meaning, but the best intentions in the world won't help if they are speaking different languages. Imagine a marriage in which the husband only speaks Polish and the wife only speaks Portuguese. Plenty of frustrations are going to be in that marriage (especially since the Polish phrase for "I'm sorry, but I don't understand you" sounds very similar to the Portuguese phrase for "You've got the brains of a refrigerator and the face of a frog").

In his book *The Five Love Languages*, marriage counselor Dr. Gary Chapman says that people tend to show love and feel loved predominately in one of five ways:

1. Acts of Service
2. Giving Gifts
3. Words of Encouragement
4. Quality Time
5. Physical Touch

If you are trying to communicate love to your spouse in a way that comes naturally for you (by giving thoughtful gifts even without an occasion), that might not be noticed by your spouse if he or she senses love in another way (such as verbal expressions of affection and encouragement).

This "language barrier" often creates huge misunderstandings in marriage:

• Wife (who speaks the "quality time" language) is

thinking: "My husband must not love me any-more. He is never at home spending time with me. He loves his work more than he loves me.

- Meanwhile, back at the office, the husband (who speaks "acts of service" language) is thinking: "This job is killing me. I'd really rather be at home with my wife, but I've got to keep working hard because I want her to know how much I love her."

Who is at fault here? We wouldn't want to take sides, so we'll just say that it is either nobody or both of them. But there is a problem that needs to be cleared up. The wife needs to recognize that her husband is communicating his love for her in the way that he knows how, and she needs to appreciate his love from that perspective. And the husband needs to realize that his paycheck isn't all that romantic and cuddly to his wife, so he needs to express his love for her in a way that she will understand better.

Learning to speak a foreign language isn't easy. At first

it seems awkward. You aren't sure what to say or how to say it. It sounds funny, and you can get a little embarrassed. But if you are in a foreign country trying to speak the indigenous language, your sincere attempts will be appreciated, even if your pronunciation is abrasive.

The same is true when you are "learning" to speak the love language that your spouse speaks. Because it is different from what is natural for you, it may seem awkward. Maybe you won't be exactly sure what you should say and do. But your spouse will recognize the attempt, and your efforts will be appreciated. And as you spend more time speaking that new language, you'll get better at it.

Find out what love language your spouse is speaking, and become very fluent in it. When you do, you might even discover that your spouse is multilingual and speaks several different love languages. Then you can start learning the other dialects as well.

- See how good you can get at learning to speak the language that your spouse understands.

- When it comes to love, actions speak louder than words—but make sure your spouse knows what your actions are saying.

- Thoughtful intentions don't count for anything unless you follow through on them.

- Sometimes the best way to say "I love you" is to pronounce it: "I'm sorry."

- A marriage counselor is usually just an interpreter for two spouses who don't speak the same language.

God and our conscience
know our secrets.
Let them correct them.

Mark the Ascetic

TEN

A GOOD KIND
OF SURPRISE

There are good surprises and there are bad surprises. Good surprises are things like an unexpected raise, a good report card from one of the kids, a clean dental checkup, and the Cubs winning the World Series. (Okay, that would be more of a miracle than a surprise, but you get the idea.)

There are good surprises in your marriage as well, such as your husband taking out the garbage on his own, or your wife actually showing interest in a televised football game. But marriages are also filled with bad surprises, and we're not just talking about the birthday party your spouse secretly arranged for you on your fortieth birthday—when you told your friends you were only thirty-nine.

No, a bad surprise is much more sinister and destructive. It's when you make a pretty big decision without consulting your spouse (especially if the decision involves money). A bad surprise is telling your wife, "I'm going out tonight," and she has no idea why. It's telling your husband something he was clueless about, and then criticizing him for not reading your mind.

There are even bigger bad surprises that usually involve your spouse discovering a secret you've been concealing (hint: it's not that present you bought for Christmas). But we don't want to dwell on the negative, because this is a chapter about good surprises.

A sure way to spice up your marriage is to plan surprises for your spouse. He or she needs to understand that the joy of surprise didn't end when you got married. You're still capable of making her smile with an unexpected bouquet of flowers. You still know how much he loves it when you take him to a movie that features explosions rather than dialogue.

You want certain areas of your life to be predictable. (Your integrity is a good example.) But when it comes to your marriage, learn to be the master of surprise.

. . .IN THE SMALL STUFF

- Express your love by sending your spouse a note through the mail.

- Offer to take the kids out for the evening so your wife can enjoy some free hours.

- Sit down with your wife after dinner, look her in the eye, and say, "Let's talk."

- Sit down with your husband after dinner, look him in the eye, and say, "Let's have sex."

God stands fast as your rock,
steadfast as your safeguard,
sleepless as your watcher,
valiant as your champion.

Charles Spurgeon

SPIRITUAL GROWTH

ELEVEN

LET GOD COME BETWEEN YOU

Some say that nothing should come between a husband and a wife: not kids, not career, not finances, not anything. We disagree, sort of. Nothing should come between a husband and a wife that acts like a wedge to divide them and drive them apart. This could happen with any of the circumstances of married life.

But one thing that can come between a husband and wife can actually bring them closer instead of separating them. This is not a spatial enigma. When God is between you and your spouse, He can do exactly that.

When God is in the middle of a marriage, then the husband and wife can be closer to each other because they share a spiritual bond. They are connected to each other through God. A genuine spiritual connection with God is stronger than any other force on earth. Nothing can separate it. And when you are linked with your spouse through that God-connection, your marriage can withstand the circumstances of life that might make other marriages falter.

God is the only priority of your life that should be higher than your spouse. We don't mean to belittle the importance of your spouse by saying that he or she holds the Number Two position. After all, finishing in second place behind God isn't all that bad. And actually, your spouse shouldn't mind, because you will be a much better marriage partner if you follow God's principles for life.

When you think about it, God would make the perfect spouse. He is loving, forgiving, patient, kind, and thoughtful.

Obviously, your spouse falls far short of that standard, and so do you. But you both have a chance of becoming more like that if both of you put God at the center of your marriage and work at reflecting those divine attributes.

God deserves a place in your marriage, and it is right between the two of you.

. . .IN THE SMALL STUFF

- Egos can make your marriage overcrowded, but God won't.

- Your marriage will do much better if you include the One who designed it.

- God is always the glue that holds you and your spouse together; sometimes He is the referee that keeps you from strangling each other.

- God should be what you have most in common with your spouse.

The earnest prayer of
a righteous person has
great power and wonderful results.

James 5:16

TWELVE

PRAYER HOLDS YOU TOGETHER

Prayer is one of the most powerful forces in your marriage for two reasons. First, it involves you with God's actions on your behalf. Second, prayer will bring you and your spouse together like nothing else in heaven or on earth.

Wow. Those are two pretty big statements. Are we saying that prayer gives God a reason to do good stuff for you and your marriage? Not exactly. God can't love you any more than He does now, because God is incapable of anything except ultimate, unconditional love. God always has your best interest in mind, and that includes your marriage.

At the same time, you and your spouse may be excluding God from your marriage—not deliberately, mind you—but in a passive sense, because you fail to communicate with God through prayer.

Because your heavenly Father loves you so much, He is always there for you, and He does things to protect and prosper you even when you're unaware of Him. That's why we always say that even in the small stuff of your life, there are no coincidences.

When you pray, however, you invite God to do even more, by actively engaging His power in your life. What prayer does in a simple and powerful way is to tell God that you desire His direct involvement in every detail of your life and the lives of those you really care about.

The reason prayer is such an effective way to bring you and your spouse together is that it puts both of you in touch with the One who loves you most and who wants your marriage to succeed even more than you do. When you pray as a couple, you will be carried above the daily routines and pressures that can sometimes bring a marriage down. You will have confidence that God will hear your prayers and give you the strength and wisdom you need.

. . .IN THE SMALL STUFF

- Prayer really does change things, especially you.

- The couple that prays together stays together.

- Prayer is the way we talk to God, and He's always listening.

- Prayer moves the hands that hold the world.

- Before all else fails, pray.

Successful marriage is always a triangle:
a man, a woman, and God.

Cecil Myers

THIRTEEN

READING THE
MARRIAGE MANUAL

The strength of your marriage will increase as you have more in common with your spouse. But what you share in common must be more than just a favorite flavor of cheesecake or matching "his and hers" pajamas. Oh sure, those things are great if you are splitting a dessert at a restaurant or posing by the fireplace for the Christmas card picture, but they won't do much good at getting you through the tough times in life.

Strong marriages are those where the wife and husband share a similar faith and have consistent values and philosophies. You didn't start out this way as a couple. While you may have had some similarities in your upbringing and backgrounds, you each came into your marriage with your own distinctive sets of beliefs and opinions. Your actions (and reactions) were the product of your life experience before your marriage. During marriage, however, you can work at refining your individual perspectives in the context of what the two of you believe as a couple.

We aren't saying that you and your spouse should each abandon your personal opinions for a kind of generic mental marital mush. But together you should be building a set of values and beliefs that characterize and define your marriage. The Bible is a great place to start the process.

Imagine what the checkout line would be like if your bookstore announced the publication and sale of an ancient book of wisdom that contained the secrets for a successful life. In fact, the Bible is that ancient tome, and every year more copies are sold of the Bible than any other book. While it is worthwhile reading for you or your spouse individually, consider how your marriage could be strengthened as you both read about God's principles for:

- loving marriage relationships
- raising children
- financial matters
- dealing with friends and strangers
- character development
- spiritual growth

Sometimes when couples start to read the Bible together, they feel a sense of awkwardness. The Bible seems a little old-fashioned in our high tech society. (If that is what's bothering you, then pull the Scripture up off the Internet, and read it together off your computer monitor.) But you do a lot of things together and discuss them afterward, such as analyzing the movie when you are driving home; reading the Bible doesn't have to be any different. Read a passage from the Bible and then talk about it with each other. If you are having trouble getting started, then use a devotional guide that includes an explanation of the passage.

The frequency of reading the Bible together is not as important as establishing the habit. Whether it is once a day at bedtime or once a week on Saturday morning doesn't matter (although you won't get into an actual habit if it is only once a year on Groundhog Day). And the habit is not for the sake of simply creating a ritual or tradition in your marriage. (You could have a tradition of taking out the garbage can together, but it doesn't seem all that worthwhile.) The purpose of reading the Bible with your spouse is to discover, together, spiritual principles that will strengthen both your relationship with God and your relationship with each other.

. . .IN THE SMALL STUFF

- The wife and husband who have a Bible that is falling apart probably have a marriage that isn't.

- Other marriage books can give you information,

but go to the Bible if you are interested in transformation.

- The Bible can take your marriage from where it is and help you get it where it needs to go.

- Owning a family Bible won't help your marriage. Reading it will.

- God won't be surprised when your marriage succeeds (but there may be a surprised mother-in-law).

This is the church of the living God,
which is the pillar and support of the truth.

1 Timothy 3:15

FOURTEEN

CHURCH DIFFERENCES

Drive around any town and you'll see lots of different churches: Baptist churches, Presbyterian churches, Methodist churches, Independent Bible churches, Catholic churches, Pentecostal churches, Orthodox churches, and Lutheran churches. It can all be rather confusing.

If you're not confused, and church makes perfect sense to you, then you probably "grew up" in a particular church, and your parents went there before you, and your grandparents before them, and when your ancestors came over on the *Mayflower*. . .well, you get the picture. Our theory is that the longer you and your family have attended a particular church or denomination, the more convinced you are that your church is the only "normal" church, and your "doctrinal" viewpoints are the best.

So what do you do when two people from two different churches get married, and each one thinks his or her church is the best? Where do they go to church? Maybe you haven't experienced conflicts in this area, but it can be a real point of contention, which isn't the way it's supposed to be. Church was never meant to be competitive. Nor was it meant to be a place where we divide. God designed church to be a place where we come together.

It's fine that we have different churches with different names and different ways of doing things. Differences are good! It shows that the universal church, comprised of all believers everywhere, is a diverse bunch.

But we should never let our differences separate us. God doesn't see us that way. The Bible says that God sees no distinction between men and women, rich and poor, slave and free, Baptist and Catholic. When we follow His Son, Jesus Christ, He sees us all as one.

So don't let church differences come between you and your spouse. Pray and ask God for wisdom. Then choose a church that best fits you both. And remember what you give to your church is more important than what you get out of church.

. . .IN THE SMALL STUFF

- The church is more than a building. It's a living, breathing organism.

- Go to church for the right reasons—convenience isn't one of them.

- Don't look for excuses to change churches.

- There's nothing wrong with attending the church your family of origin attends, but don't make that the primary reason for selecting a church.

Marriages are made in heaven.
So are thunderstorms and hurricanes.

Anonymous

FIFTEEN

GOD KNOWS WHAT
YOUR MARRIAGE NEEDS

Whom can you go to when you are having problems in your marriage? A friend, a relative, or maybe a marriage counselor. These outsiders may be of some limited help, but their analyses will be shallow. They haven't had the opportunity to know what is really going on in your home.

God is the best marriage counselor you will ever find. Look at what He has to offer:

- He has known both you and your spouse since birth. He knows your personalities. He knows your quirks.

- He has knowledge of what has been happening in your marriage since the two of you exchanged rings at the wedding ceremony.

- He is available to you at your convenience. You won't have trouble making an appointment.

- He doesn't charge $225 an hour.

- You don't have to go to His office. You can use your own couch.

God knows exactly what your marriage needs. And He'll be glad to tell you if you talk to Him about it. Don't expect to hear a booming voice from heaven (with a Sigmund Freud accent). God will most likely speak to you through the Bible, in the quietness of your thoughts. And don't expect that

God will find that all of the problems are your spouse's fault. He may want you to make some changes.

God wants your marriage to be a success, and He knows how to make it that way. Listen to what He has to say.

. . .In the Small Stuff

- Your spouse may be inattentive, but God isn't.

- If you're having problems in your marriage, stop complaining about it and start praying about it.

- God handles the eternal plans of the universe, so you should be able to trust Him with the problems of your marriage.

- Pray for your spouse—but be ready for God to start changing you.

Growth is the
only evidence of life.

John Henry Newman

PERSONAL GROWTH

SIXTEEN

SPACE PLANNING:
MAKING ROOM TO GROW

The number one relationship killer is "the tendency to control others." That's what Alan Loy McGinnis wrote in his book *The Friendship Factor*. We agree. Everybody has this tendency in some way, but those who let their need for control get out of control risk ruining an otherwise healthy relationship.

Control is a subtle thing. Sometimes you control because you think you know what's best for the other person, when in fact it may just be your opinion or preference. Other times you control because you don't want someone else—especially someone you care a great deal about—to change. You're afraid that they will "get ahead" of you or perhaps—heaven forbid—force you out of your comfort zone.

Now controlling someone may be okay if that someone is changing for the worse (and even then, control isn't the best tactic), but why would you want to stop someone from changing for the better? Yet that's exactly what we do, perhaps because it threatens our own complacency.

We express our controlling tendencies in many ways, mostly by little barbs of criticism. And usually we don't know we're doing it. That's why it's important to take steps in the other direction, away from control to freedom.

Dr. McGinnis calls this "creating space in your relationship." Here are his five recommendations on how you do this:

1. Be cautious with criticism.
2. Use the language of acceptance.
3. Encourage your spouse to be unique.
4. Allow for solitude.
5. Encourage other relationships.

If you need any more advice in your space planning, here's what the Bible says: "Love is patient and kind. Love is not jealous."

. . .In the Small Stuff

- Let love, not jealousy, characterize your marriage.

- Don't confuse lust and love. Lust is self-serving; love serves others.

- Ask God to help you love your mate without expecting anything in return.

- If your spouse hasn't been alone for a while, create the opportunity.

- Don't be a nosy spouse.

My definition of marriage. . .
it resembles a pair of shears,
so joined that they cannot be separated;
often moving in opposite directions,
yet always punishing anyone who
comes between them.

Sydney Smith

SEVENTEEN

OPPOSITES ATTRACT

Marriages are the combination of two people with strengths and weaknesses that usually offset each other. The wife will have some strong points, and with those she can compensate for the weaknesses of her husband. And the husband will excel in some areas that are difficult for his wife.

If the strengths of each spouse in your marriage counterbalance the limitations of the other, you've got a strong combination. Together you'll be able to manage life's circumstances, because one or the other of you will step up to the plate, depending upon which of you is best suited to handle the situation. This teamwork will give you confidence in your marriage, as well as admiration for the strengths of your spouse.

This teamwork concept in marriage works great, but you shouldn't adhere strictly to it. If you each only do what you are good at, you'll end up being two people who are each operating at fifty percent capacity:

- Don't rely so heavily on the strengths of your spouse that you stop working to improve those areas in which you are weak.

- Don't take on every situation that falls within the areas of your strengths. Leave some for your spouse.

Strengths are good, and you each need to have them. But weaknesses are good, too, because they give you an opportunity for self-improvement. Instead of two people each operating at fifty percent, your marriage can be comprised of two people each functioning at seventy-five percent. And a marriage operating at 150 percent proficiency will be a real success.

. . .IN THE SMALL STUFF

- Marriage is a team sport.

- Keep falling in love with your spouse's strengths, and keep forgetting the faults.

- If you can live with your own flaws, then you can certainly tolerate those of your spouse.

- At the wedding you say, "I do." After that, you should be saying, "We will."

- Marriage is the realization that you are incomplete without your spouse.

There is a time for everything,
a season for every activity under heaven.

Ecclesiastes 3:1

EIGHTEEN

LESSONS FROM NATURE

Just like there are seasons in nature, there are seasons in life. Even your marriage is not exempt from this principle. As you progress in your married life, both you and your spouse will go through seasons of change and growth (those are the fun seasons). You will also have seasons of dormancy and death—not fun at all, but a necessary part of life.

Here's our take on the seasons of life. As you ponder these, keep in mind that sometimes you will experience them as a married couple, and sometimes as individuals.

SPRING
This is the season of joy, when new growth occurs. Your marriage starts in this season. You children are born in this season. This is when God seems very close in both the big and small stuff of your marriage.

SUMMER
Ah, those lazy, crazy days of summer. This season is made for relaxing, vacationing, and renewing. This is when your marriage seems like it's in cruise control with no concerns or worries.

FALL
Summer can lull you into complacency. You may even begin to take your marriage for granted. But gradually, some of the things you've worked so hard to achieve start turning sour. Fall is the season of disappointments and unfulfilled expectations. This is the time when you need to take stock of your relationship. Make corrections when necessary and give

thanks for the good things you have.

WINTER

Doubt, disasters, disease, and death characterize this season. Nobody willingly enters this time of life, but it will come at different times in your married life. This is the time when God will seem far away and you will feel all alone. That's precisely why you need to call on Him for help and comfort. Make no mistake about it, God will answer—not by removing your winter, but by giving you the strength to get through it.

You may be taken by surprise when a brand new spring melts your coldest winter. But it will. Just like nature needs every season to continue its course and produce its bounty, you need to go through every season in order for your marriage to thrive.

- Without winter there can be no spring.

- Unlike the seasons in nature, the seasons of your life are not predictable.

- Like a wise farmer watching over his crops, expect the best but prepare for the worst.

- The seasons of your life don't come in equal time periods, but they all have equal value.

- The greatest growth always occurs after the toughest times.

- Never take credit for your seasons of joy and happiness; they are God's gift to you.

- God doesn't cause your seasons of doubt and disappointment, but He promises to get you through them.

- Seasons of joy should produce gratitude.

- Seasons of disappointment should produce hope.

- Sometimes it's necessary to do some self-pruning so greater growth can occur.

- As you gain experience enjoying and enduring your own seasons, be willing to help others through theirs.

Y ou've got to be careful if
you don't know where you're going,
'cause you might not get there.

Yogi Berra

NINETEEN

THE JOY OF BECOMING

A traditional part of many weddings is the lighting of the unity candle. Three candles are set in a row, with the two outside candles burning (representing the bride and groom before marriage). In a symbolic gesture to represent their new union, the bride and groom each take their respective candle, and together they light the center candle. Then they blow out the flames on their personal candles, and only the center candle remains lit. It is a nice demonstration of the biblical principle that "the two shall become one."

But the symbolism of this unity candle hoopla should not be taken to its extreme. Your own personal life and identity are not snuffed out the moment you become married. You do not lose your individuality, and you are not relegated from a whole person to just half of a couple.

Marriage brings a new dimension of togetherness into your life, but it should not stifle your personal distinctiveness. As an individual, you must still develop and improve yourself. (The same is true of your spouse, but for right now we are just talking about you.)

Don't let marriage stop your growth as a person. Apart from your spouse, you need to continue to improve spiritually, mentally, socially, and physically. Continue your education; get in the habit of reading; pursue a hobby that interests you; develop new friendships; and maintain that exercise program (or at least get one started). It will be great if your spouse can join you in some of these activities, but assume responsibility for your own development.

You don't stop being a person when you become

married, so don't stop developing your mind and body. Enjoy the journey of becoming a little better each day. You'll be a good role model for your children (and you might even be setting a challenge for your spouse to keep up with you).

. . .IN THE SMALL STUFF

- Make your marriage better by improving yourself.

- If you always stay the same as you were on the day you were married, you'll have a boring life.

- Work on changing your shortcomings even though your spouse overlooks them.

- Your marriage began with the two of you becoming one. Don't spend the rest of your lives trying to figure out which one.

Marriage was ordained for
a remedy and to increase the world
and for the man to help the woman
and the woman the man,
with all love and kindness.

William Tyndale

TWENTY

WHEN YOUR GROWTH SPURTS ARE OUT OF SYNC

There will be times in your marriage when one of you will grow at a different rate than your spouse. This could happen for a number of reasons:

- You get a promotion at work, while your spouse feels stuck at home or in a dead-end job.

- You join a Bible study and start growing spiritually at a faster rate than your spouse.

- You start an exercise routine that helps you get into shape while your spouse just feels "fat."

- You go to a men's/women's retreat and come back from the mountaintop with an undeniable "glow."

- You go back to school and take some classes that challenge you intellectually.

Even though you are growing, and your spouse completely approves of the changes, your spouse may have some feelings of resentment that can undermine your marriage in profound ways. Resentment may cause your spouse to minimize or even discount your growth and achievements. Rather than being proud of you, your spouse will literally try to bring you down to his or her level.

In our experience, the antidote to resentment is encouragement. If you find yourself feeling this resentment, remember: Rather than bringing your spouse down to your level through resentment, use encouragement to raise yourself to your spouse's level.

. . .In the Small Stuff

- Learn to appreciate each other's growth spurts.

- Never criticize your spouse for trying something new.

- When possible, invite your spouse to participate in your season of growth.

- You can't force your spouse to grow, but you can be a gentle encourager.

- Rather than an accident, make growth a habit in your life.

Before I got married,
I had six theories about bringing up children;
now I have six children and no theories.

Lord Rochester

CHILDREN

TWENTY-ONE

WHEN AND HOW MANY

Hopefully, the subject of children will be discussed between the two of you before the minister says, "I now pronounce you husband and wife." It is important to have previously reached an opinion on this issue because:

- Some aunt at the wedding reception will be asking about it.

- Before you return home from the honeymoon, your mother will be knitting little booties.

- You'll freak out when you're shopping for your first home if your choice is a two-bedroom cottage but your spouse insists on an abandoned army barracks (because "we could never fit our twelve kids in two bedrooms").

These issues of "when" and "how many" are very personal for each couple. We won't meddle in your marriage by suggesting a number or a timetable, but we've got a few guidelines:

- Discuss the subject of children with your spouse before you crank up the baby-manufacturing mechanisms. The two of you may have completely different perspectives (especially if you were an only child, and your spouse came from a family where they named the kids in alphabetical order and stopped when they couldn't think of a "Q" name). Remember to discuss your philosophies on discipline.

- Postpone the final decision of how many children you'll eventually have until after your first one is born. Take it one at a time (with the exception of multiple births, and then take it groups at a time). See how you like being parents before you multiply the experience.

- Don't wait for the "perfect time" to have children. It will never come. You will never be prepared financially. You will never have a perfect schedule. You will never have everything ready.

- Don't feel pressured by anyone. Well, you will be pressured, but don't give in to it. If all of your friends start having babies, you are going to feel ostracized. You'll find that the conversations center on disposable diapers, car seats, and breast pumps (and that's what the dads are talking about); you'll be left out if you're still interested in vacations and the stock market. Don't increase the population of your family just so you won't be left out of conversations. (Take our word for it, anything that could be said about breast pumps is not all that interesting.)

- A baby won't solve the problems of your marriage. If your marriage is already on shaky ground, the addition of a child could be like an earthquake.

Children bring a lot of surprises into a family. You can't plan for the surprises, but you can do a little advance planning about the children.

. . .IN THE SMALL STUFF

- Children are like mosquitoes. When they stop making noise, you know they are getting into something.

- An alarm clock is a device for waking up adults who don't have small children.

- You think you know a lot about raising children until you have them.

- Before you have your own children, you consider a juvenile delinquent to be the product of poor parenting. After you have kids of your own, you put the blame on the child's own defiant attitude.

- There is a huge difference between pets and babies. If you don't already know the difference, then don't volunteer to babysit for anyone.

Teach your children to choose the right path,
and when they are older,
they will remain upon it.

Proverbs 22:6

TWENTY-TWO

PARENTING 101

Parenting is one of the toughest jobs on the planet. By contrast, rocket science is a piece of cake. Managing a large company with hundreds of employees? A cinch. Running a marathon? No comparison. Being a parent is a lot more demanding. It will tax your brain, push you to the limit of your abilities, and take you to the edge of your physical strength like nothing else. But what a ride!

Parenting is not for the timid, but that shouldn't dissuade you from joining the club. The joys of parenting far outweigh the heartaches (as a parent, you'll have plenty of both), and somehow at the end of the day, even though you are totally exhausted and emotionally spent, you decide it's worth doing again tomorrow.

Successful parents seem to have three things in common:

1. They love their children unconditionally.
2. They take the time to get to know their children individually.
3. They put God at the center of their family ritually.

If you're part of a two-parent household, congratulations. That's becoming an increasingly rare commodity these days. Take advantage of your strength in numbers by sharing the parenting duties. Approach the job like a team approaches the Big Game. Your individual efforts won't count as much as you and your spouse parenting together, in sync. And always show love and respect for each other, whether or not the kids are in the room.

If you are a single parent, or a parent with marriage challenges, don't use the kids as an excuse. Don't force them to "pick sides." For the sake of your kids—and more importantly, for your sake—work out your differences. If God seems distant, invite Him into your family through prayer and Bible study. This may sound like a trite answer to some big problems, but you will be amazed at what a huge difference Bible reading and prayer will make to your family.

...IN THE SMALL STUFF

- Husbands, the best way to show love to your kids is to love their mother.

- Wives, the best way to show love to your kids is to respect their father.

- In order to effectively guide your children, you have to thoroughly know them.

- Remember it was God, not Darwin, who designed the family.

- Where your family is concerned, there's no such thing as chance.

Children are unpredictable.
You never know what inconsistency
they're going to catch you in next.

Franklin P. Jones

TWENTY-THREE

THE CARE AND COACHING
OF TEENAGERS

The teenagers in your family need a lot of certain things: food, privacy, acne medication, clothes, Internet time, and more food. And they don't hesitate to proclaim their demands for this stuff. (Except they're usually secretive about requests for the acne medication.) But they will never ask for the thing that they need the most: a consistent, positive role model for marriage.

There are a lot of people who are competing for

influence over your teenager's life. Don't think that you are out of the competition just because you are a parent. You should be leading the race. You have the greatest impact of all on your teenager's life, but whether the impact is positive or negative will depend upon how well you do your job.

Teenagers have a knack for spotting hypocrisy. They may not see it as easily in their sports heroes or with the entertainment celebrities, but they can sure spot it in your life and marriage. (It's not your fault. Your teenager just doesn't have the opportunity to see the pro athletes and the celebrities in the kitchen at the end of a hard week.) But you have the opportunity to pass along to your teenager great impressions of marriage (of which there are too few examples in the media) if you consistently show love, courtesy, and kindness to your spouse.

Even if you do a fantastic job of raising your children, don't expect that you'll receive a gold medal from your teenager at the awards ceremony for the Parental Olympics. Children, at least while they are teenagers, do not give that kind of recognition and acknowledgment to their parents. Your award will come later, when your children get married and model their marriages after what they learned from you.

. . .IN THE SMALL STUFF

- If you want your children to end up with happy marriages, show them one.

- The reason that teenagers think they know all the answers about love and marriage is because they haven't heard all of the questions.

- If you want your teenagers to spend more time at home, you have to make your home a pleasant place to be. (And it helps to let the air out of the tires on their cars.)

- The best thing you can do for your teenager is to love your spouse.

Our children are our most important guests,
who enter into our home,
ask for careful attention,
stay for a while and then
leave to follow their own way.

Henri Nouwen

TWENTY-FOUR

LEAVE YOUR KIDS BEFORE
THEY LEAVE YOU

It's important to prepare your kids to leave the nest long before they actually do—by leaving them first. No, you don't drop them off on some benevolent stranger's doorstep (although you may feel like it sometimes). You do everything you can to build in them a spirit of independence, something like an inner scaffolding that will hold up long after the outer scaffolding of their home and family has been taken down. This inner scaffolding needs to be built on the foundation of God and His Word. By teaching and modeling small things measured out every day, you will better prepare your kids along the way.

Too many parents think they "own" their kids. Nothing could be farther from the truth. Children are a gift from God, given to parents to nurture and love. As Henri Nouwen wrote, they are "guests" in your home for a while, and the best thing you can do is help them "grow to the freedom that permits them to stand on their own feet, physically, mentally, and spiritually, and allow them to move away in their own direction."

It's true! Think about the guests you have had in your home. You don't treat them like possessions. You do everything you can to improve the quality of their lives while they are with you. You don't kick them out of the house, but neither do you say, "Don't ever leave us." When it's time for your guests to leave, you send them off better for having been in your care.

Leaving your children involves nothing more than letting them go and giving them to God. If you do this before they leave you, then they will go with your blessing, your prayers, and your love.

. . .IN THE SMALL STUFF

- It may be years before your children thank you for leaving them and letting them go, but they will eventually show their gratitude.

- Children are a privilege, not a right.

- You are more likely to lose a child you grip too tightly than one you release lovingly.

- It's easier to give your children to God if you realize they are His to begin with.

Everybody knows how to raise children,
except people who have them.

P. J. O'Rourke

TWENTY-FIVE

No Kids?
Know Kids!

What if your marriage doesn't include children? Is your family of two substandard? Are you outcasts in a society that caters to familial units with the "family-package" for everything from amusement park tickets to buckets of fried chicken? Are you doomed to experience less than God's best because you hang only two Christmas stockings from your mantle? Absolutely not!

Your marriage is not incomplete if you have no children,

but it will be if you don't know children.

If you are without offspring of your own, then you are in the perfect position to develop a meaningful relationship with children whom you could help. Maybe you could fill a grandparent role for some children who have no grandparents in their family. Or, just in case we offended you by suggesting that you could be in a geriatric category, maybe you could fill the role of the hip older brother or sister for a teenager.

The benefit of your relationship with some children won't be all one-sided. Sure, the kids will get the advantage of your friendship, but you will benefit too. A child can bring a fresh perspective into your life. You and your spouse will look at things differently, and you'll have a greater sense of wonder and amazement. (If you don't believe us, just go to an amusement park by yourselves, and then go back with a six-year-old.) The benefits for you will depend upon the age of the children with whom you build a friendship. (Teenagers can give you fashion suggestions so you won't dress like the stiffs on CNN.)

You have the rare opportunity to make a difference in the life of a child without some of the routine and hardships that are associated with parenthood. Don't waste this opportunity. There are some children out there who need you.

. . .IN THE SMALL STUFF

- If you've got time, you've got exactly what a child needs.

- People who have a hard time understanding teenagers maybe aren't listening to them.

- Children may feel comfortable in your house because they don't in their own.

- You may need to make the footsteps for a child to follow.

- Always have a close relationship with a young child (because you never know when you'll need some help with your computer, VCR, or other technology).

Out of ego needs,
we put our best foot forward
for the people we care the least about,
and our worst foot forward
for the people who mean the most to us.

Lane Adams

FAMILY AND FRIENDS

TWENTY-SIX

YOU MARRIED AN ENTIRE FAMILY

Marriage is still popular because most people have no idea what they're getting into. We have this mistaken notion that marriage is an ideal proposition between two people who are hopelessly in love. We dream our dreams and make our plans based on the assumption that we will build our lives together, completely on our own, a cord of three strands that includes just the two of us and God.

How wonderful that we believe that to be true! If we really knew what was about to happen, we might never enter the bonds of holy matrimony.

The thing is, it is just the two of you and God in your marriage. But outside that cozy little marriage cord of three is a bunch of other cords. . .and scraps of twine, pieces of string, and lots of rope. These are your parents, your in-laws, your brothers and sisters, uncles and aunts, nephews, nieces, and cousins. Marriage would be so much simpler if all you had to worry about was the two of you, and the only one you had to please was God. But that's not the way it is. As soon as you say, "I do," you commit yourself to your husband or wife—and his or her entire family.

If you're lucky, your families will give you room and time before cautiously entering your starry-eyed world. However, if you're like most couples, you'll barely have time to warm up the sheets in your new bed before the in-laws on both sides invade your fortress of solitude.

We're not saying that your extended family is bad— and we're not saying they don't mean well. We're not saying they should mind their own business. . .well, maybe we are, and maybe they should! But the reality is that you have no control over what your families are going to do, so you might as well get together on a plan to deal with these other people you married.

Actually, that's the first step. Realize that you married each other, but that you also married into each other's family. Understanding this is half the battle. Second, accept the fact that despite information to the contrary, your families really do mean well. When your husband's mother calls, it's not that she doesn't trust you to take care of her baby like she has all these years. She simply misses her son, and without coming right out and saying it, she wants to know if he misses her, too.

When your wife's sister drops by at the most inappropriate moments, it doesn't mean she's nosy. She's just lonely and needs some contact with her little sis'.

And when Uncle Jack stares at your beautiful wife at the family reunion, don't get upset. It's Uncle Jack, for crying out loud. He stares at the Morton's Salt girl on the grocery store shelf.

If you don't like being surprised by relatives, try some preemptive measures. Call your mother (and while you're at it, call your mother-in-law). Take your sister-in-law out to lunch, and buy Uncle Jack a case of Morton's Salt. Get to know your in-laws, which not only shows them respect for helping to raise and nurture your spouse, but also gives you insights into the person you married. The better you get to know that family, the better you will get to know your husband or wife.

. . .IN THE SMALL STUFF

- It may not take a village to raise a child, but it does take a family.

- If you don't let your family get under your skin, they won't bug you so much.

- Keep in mind that all families think other families are a little strange.

- Remember that you and your spouse are part of someone else's extended family.

- Treat your spouse's family the way you want them to treat you.

- Your friends may see right through your flattery, but your family loves it.

No husband is really successful
until his mother-in-law admits it.

Anonymous

TWENTY-SEVEN

OUT WITH THE IN-LAWS

Every husband and wife can learn a lot about "in-law" relationships from Adam and Eve. Adam and Eve didn't have parents, so neither of them had in-laws butting into their marriage. And that is the lesson that can be learned from Adam and Eve. Don't let your parents be the crabgrass in your Garden of Eden. (Okay, we realize that we pushed the analogy too far, but our point is still valid.)

Once you become married, your relationship with

your parents needs to change. Yes, you are still their child, but now you need to have an independent life. This might be a difficult transition for them. They remember that for most of your life you were dependent upon them. Hey, they used to change your diapers. ("It only seems like yesterday we were powdering your tiny hiney.") Well, a lot of years have passed since "yesterday," and the size of your hiney proves it. Opinions and recommendations from parents are fine when you ask for them, but otherwise parents need to keep their viewpoints, and their baby powder, to themselves.

Of course, you have to be careful that you are not encouraging parental intrusion into your marriage by your actions. You can't be calling them and asking their "objective opinion" on issues over which you and your spouse are arguing. Your parents aren't going to be objective. They're going to take your side. And they're going to think that you are dependent upon them if you have to keep borrowing money from them. If you have to borrow money, get it from the bank (because the bank president isn't going to foreclose on a loan just because your spouse made an insensitive comparison between your mom's Thanksgiving stuffing and sawdust).

When you get married, your primary loyalty shifts to your spouse. It's the two of you, on your own, for better or worse. Keep the parents at a respectful distance from the personal matters of your marriage.

. . .IN THE SMALL STUFF

- If marriage were illegal, then only outlaws would have in-laws.

- If you have to run home to mommy, then you weren't mature enough to get married.

- A comedian gets a lot of laughs at the expense of his mother-in-law. Don't you be a comedian.

- If you keep your parents out of your marriage, then you'll love having them in your family.

I'm the kind of friend
you can depend on.
I'm always around
when I need you.

Anonymous

TWENTY-EIGHT

THE OLD GANG AND
THE OLD HANGOUTS

For a guy, being single has its advantages, and these go beyond the obvious ones involving laundry and hygiene. A single guy doesn't have nearly as much responsibility as a married man does. He can play golf as often as he likes, eat out at the same greasy spoon any time he wants, and go to the game with a buddy on the spur of the moment.

For a woman, the single life also has its appeal. For one thing, your apartment stays neater and smells better. You can eat with your girlfriends at any number of sidewalk cafés around town. And when that new art exhibition of the French Romantics comes to the city, you don't think twice about going with a couple of friends.

Another advantage for both single men and women is that generally it's easier to talk to a member of your own sex than it is to engage in meaningful conversation with someone of the opposite sex. But that was then, and this is now. Once you were single, but now you're married, and you just can't associate in the same way with the same people you used to enjoy and do the same things you used to do.

This is where a lot of married people make a mistake. They like being married, but somehow they believe that it's still okay to hang out with the old gang at the old hangouts. In fact, it's better than okay, it's great, like a spoonful of sherbet between the heavy courses of marriage.

No, it's not great. It's self-centered. It's refusing to give your marriage first priority. How do you expect to grow together as a couple if you keep going back to those old friends and those old places? Your marriage needs your full attention and devotion. You need to find common interests and friends and build your activities around them. . .together. You won't lose anything except your old way of doing things. And you will gain new experiences and new perspectives in a way you could never do when you were single.

. . .IN THE SMALL STUFF

- Remember one of the reasons you got married: You wanted to share your life with another person.

- Find some new hangouts you can enjoy as a couple.

- When you talk to old friends, tell them how much you enjoy being married.

- The things you and your spouse have in common bring stability to your marriage. Your diversity makes it fun.

Life's most persistent and urgent question is:
What are you doing for others?

Martin Luther King

TWENTY-NINE

LOVE THY NEIGHBOR

The Bruce & Stan research and polling team (that's us with clipboards) has discovered an interesting fact: Married couples have a high incidence of vision loss. Our surveys show that if not properly treated, marriage restricts peripheral vision. Now, if you know anything about anatomy or physiology, you might be tempted to challenge our findings. But we aren't talking about ocular clarity. We are referring to the tendency to focus your time, energy, and resources on yourself rather than others.

Self-centeredness is a malady that can plague anyone. You don't have to be married to be self-absorbed. (Narcissists don't usually wed because they are already in love with themselves.) But marriage often causes people to get so involved in their own lives that they forget about others. It can happen without you even noticing it:

- Before you were married, you only worried about one schedule—yours. If you wanted to make time for charitable activities, you only had to check with yourself.

- With the wedding came the difficulty of collating the pages in two Day-Timers. You have less available time for others because much of your life is coordinated with your spouse.

- The scheduling problems multiply logarithmically as you have children.

- And you'll have less "free time" even when you

reach retirement. (With doctor appointments and traveling to Branson and Lawrence Welk Village, you won't even have time to see your grandson's Little League game.)

If you aren't careful, your day can be filled with worthwhile and necessary activities that benefit your household exclusively and help no one else in the larger world.

When Jesus was asked which of the Commandments was the most important, He boiled down all of the laws of the Old Testament into two requirements:

> *You must love the Lord your God with all your heart, all your soul, and all your mind. This is the first and greatest commandment. A second is equally important: Love your neighbor as yourself.*
>
> MATTHEW 22:37–39

Jesus said that loving your neighbor is as important as loving God. That must mean that we need to give it a high priority in our lives—even though our schedules are already crammed with personal activities.

Make sure that a part of your married life includes spending time with people who aren't in your family:

- Talk with the kids in your neighborhood. (Answering the door on Halloween night doesn't count.)

- Get involved with a ministry at your church.

- Volunteer in a community program.

- Send letters to friends that you haven't contacted (since you dropped them off your Christmas card list).

If you can participate in these activities with your spouse, that is great. But if the two of you cannot achieve scheduling compatibility, then you should each go it alone, because in the long run when you give to others, the blessing returns to you doublefold. But make sure you are each doing something that benefits someone else.

Life will be much more rewarding if you spend some of your valuable time doing something kind for someone else.

. . .In the Small Stuff

- Forget about random acts of kindness until you have done some intentional ones.

- You can't love your neighbors if you don't even know who they are.

- Charity begins at home, but it ought to get out of the house.

- You will get the greatest value out of the kind things that you do for free.

One of the most beautiful qualities
of true friendship is to
understand and to be understood.

Seneca

THIRTY

COMPATIBILITY
TIMES TWO

While we have suggested that you break away from the old gang once you are married, we certainly aren't telling you to abandon your friends, who can be a valuable source of strength, encouragement, and accountability. You need to foster friendships where you both gain and give those qualities. What you're going to find is that genuine friends will complement and compliment your marriage. In other words, they will add value to your life while supporting your marriage and your spouse.

Friendships are usually made on a one-to-one basis. It's only natural. But what about you and your spouse as a couple? Should you try to make friends with other couples? Absolutely. In fact, we'll go so far as to say that just as your body needs vitamins to supplement your diet, your marriage needs other couples as friends.

Quality couples will stimulate and challenge you to be better. As the bonds of friendship between you and a few other couples develop, you will grow in your marriage. You will be less likely to stay in a rut or stray down the wrong path.

If you are going to be good friends with at least one other couple, compatibility is very important. You may get along great with the husband, but if your wife can't stand his wife, the friendship will never work. The two of you may have lots in common, but if your husbands are as compatible as oil and water, your friendship as a couple is doomed to failure.

That's okay. You don't want to be and you can't be close friends with every couple you meet. If in your married life you meet two or three other couples who become close lifelong friends, consider yourselves blessed. When complete compatibility between two couples is reached—especially when all four of you love the Lord—there is no better friendship.

. . .IN THE SMALL STUFF

- Get to know an older couple so they can mentor you.

- Become close friends with another couple so they can encourage you.

- Befriend a young couple so they can learn from you.

- Don't ever let your compatibility with another couple lead to inappropriate familiarity.

- Compatible couples wisely leave the door open for other couples to join the fun.

We are frantically trying to
earn enough to buy things
we are too busy to enjoy.

Frank Clark

FINANCES

THIRTY-ONE

FISCAL INTIMACY

You can have a few secrets from your spouse. The acceptable confidential categories include: (a) plans for a surprise birthday party; (b) places for Christmas gifts that haven't been wrapped yet; (c) embarrassing nicknames that you were called in elementary school; and (d) any tattoos that were removed before the wedding.

Notice that there is no category for financial matters. Money matters must definitely be discussed with your spouse. There should be no secrets between you in this area.

If your marriage is going through financial struggles, it is unfair to both of you if only one of you knows about it. Both of you need to be aware of the problem, and you both need to be part of the solution. If only one spouse is aware of the difficulty, then the other spouse might unintentionally increase the problem. Friction and resentment will be the inevitable result (as one spouse scrimps while the other video-tapes infomercials so as not to miss the offers for tanning lotion, rotisserie cookers, or the car wax that protects the shine even if volcano lava splashes on the hood).

Does this mean you have to present each other with daily cash receipts for your Starbucks coffee? Of course not (although the expense of a twice daily "latté" habit may require a bank loan after a few months). Does it mean that both of you have to sign every check? No, because one of you probably hates this task and the other might enjoy paying the bills.

You both don't need to know the exact balance in each account, but you both need to have a general idea of how much money you've got and where it goes (and how much is left).

. . .IN THE SMALL STUFF

- Maybe your underwear drawer can be "off-limits" to your spouse, but the financial drawer must be accessible to both of you.

- Secrets about money can be expensive. They can cost you your marriage.

- One of you can spend money a lot faster than the other can save it. That's why communication is important.

- Don't let your financial worth be the way you measure the success of your marriage.

- If you've got a good marriage, you'll never be poor (even if you don't have any money).

This explains why a man
leaves his father and mother
and is joined to his wife,
and the two are united into one.

Genesis 2:24

THIRTY-TWO

YOURS, MINE, AND OURS

Most of us put ownership right up there with voting and apple pie. We feel that owning stuff is our inalienable right. Once we own something, no one can take it away from us.

So strong is the emotion of ownership that many people let it muddy up their marriage. We all bring stuff to a relationship, and before we marry, it's only proper to keep track of who owns what (after all, the relationship may not work out, and you want to make sure you can get back your set of Neil Diamond CDs). But once you marry, there's no need to keep inventory of your personal belongings.

No longer do you belong to yourself; you have become one with somebody else. So has your stuff. If you continue to think of your belongings as yours alone—whether they include cars, furnishings, or children (remember, you don't own them in the first place)—you will only hinder your growth as a married couple. Ownership doesn't just apply to things. You can own a habit or a certain way of doing something so strongly that you refuse to change or compromise for the good of your marriage.

A powerful spiritual principle is at work here. Before you invited God into your life, ownership was all you had. Your focus was on earthly pleasures and life habits in the here and now. When your relationship with God began, your perspective changed. You became a new person from the inside out. As a child of God, you recognize that everything you have and all that you are belong to God. Life is not about ownership now but stewardship.

Unlike an owner, who claims rights to a piece of property, a steward takes care of someone else's belongings. As a

Christian, you are compelled to carefully manage what God has given you—and that includes your marriage. Before you were married, you had yours, and she had hers. There was your stuff and there was his stuff. Now it's yours together, and everything you have belongs to God.

. . .In the Small Stuff

- In your marriage, your goal should not be to protect yourself and your belongings. Instead, you should work to protect your spouse, both physically and emotionally.

- Give up the idea of ownership in your marriage and replace it with the concept of stewardship.

- Even as a couple you can be obsessed with your stuff.

- Hold your stuff loosely, because it could all be gone tomorrow.

CREDIT MANAGER: "Do you have money in the
    bank?"
APPLICANT: "Certainly."
CREDIT MANAGER: "How much?"
APPLICANT: "I don't know. I haven't shaken it
    lately."

H.E. Martz

THIRTY-THREE

PAPER OR
PLASTIC?

Financial problems are a primary source of marital problems. And debt is the most common financial problem. And credit cards are the easiest way to get into debt.

There is nothing *wrong* with using credit cards:

- You can whip out your "gold" card to impress your friends (and they won't know you have a credit limit of only $100).

- You can accumulate free airline miles for every dollar you charge (and after charging half the gross national product, you can fly one-way to Bakersfield).

- A thin plastic card in your pants pocket is better than a wad of cash (as it avoids unsightly bulges).

Use credit cards only if you have the money to pay the bill in full at the end of the month. Otherwise, you'll be getting in debt a little bit each month. It only takes a few months like that before you'll be in a major financial crisis.

Credit cards are tempting. When you use them, it doesn't seem like you are spending real money. Swiping the card is far less painful than writing a check or pulling currency out of your wallet. That's the problem. It's too easy.

You and your spouse will have a difficult time functioning in society if you don't have credit cards. Currency will be a thing of the past when you start buying your groceries and toilet paper off the Internet. That's why both of you need to have a disciplined approach to using credit cards. Your marriage can't afford it otherwise.

. . .In the Small Stuff

- Even if the price is discounted, it's not a real bargain if you don't have the cash to pay for it.

- If you are always borrowing money, you'll be borrowing trouble for your marriage.

- You can run into debt very quickly, but it takes a long time to crawl out.

- Don't use credit cards as a matter of convenience if paying the invoice is a huge inconvenience.

- You've got a better chance of having an outstanding marriage if your bills aren't outstanding.

The goal in marriage is
not to think alike,
but to think together.

Robert C. Dodds

THIRTY-FOUR

WHO'S IN CHARGE?

Some things about marriage haven't changed since Adam proposed to Eve. For example, women have always enjoyed foot rubs, and men have never stopped to ask for directions.

At the same time, there are things about marriage that have changed, some of them in our lifetime. One of those changes has to do with finances. We grew up in the "Father Knows Best" era, when the man of the house was in charge of the money. It didn't matter whether he worked as a ditch digger or an insurance salesman, the king of the castle had to oversee the coin of the realm. That meant he paid the bills, bought the cars, and doled out the allowances. Even his wife got an allowance, so she could buy groceries and personal items, like pearl necklaces. This arrangement did not evolve from some financial study that found men to be better money managers than women. There's no verse in the Bible that says, "Husbands, pay the bills."

Today things are different. Smart men (like us) are finally recognizing that our wives are very skilled in money matters. They know how to save money and hunt for bargains far better than we do. They are logical when it comes to purchases, and they know a good investment when they see it.

King Solomon, the wisest man who ever lived, recognized these qualities in the "virtuous and capable wife" when he wrote: "She carefully watches all that goes on in her household and does not have to bear the consequences of laziness" (Proverbs 31:27).

So who should be in charge of the family finances, including paying the bills? Probably the one who's best qualified. In your household, only you can answer that.

. . .In the Small Stuff

- Isn't it interesting that some of the most popular financial advisers today are women?

- Deciding who should handle the family finances should have nothing to do with who wears the pants.

- If you are a saver and your spouse is a spender, compromise by each agreeing to do a little less of each.

- As much as possible, simplify your marriage by simplifying your finances.

- A good rule to follow: Never loan anything to friends and family unless you can live without getting it back.

M y grandfather once told me that
there are two kinds of people:
those who do the work and
those who take the credit.
He told me to try to be in the first group;
there was much less competition there.

Indira Gandhi

WORK

THIRTY-FIVE

WHO COOKS THE BACON IF BOTH BRING IT HOME?

Our society has moved far away from the role models set by Ward and June Cleaver. Their division of labor was clearly defined. June stayed in the kitchen, dressed in her polka-dot dress and embroidered apron. Ward was the breadwinner, and his domain in the home was restricted to the den where he could be found in a cardigan sweater, sitting in the leather wing chair, reviewing the contents of his briefcase.

For many marriages, the one-paycheck income is about

as antiquated as the embroidered apron. If both spouses are in the workforce, then the traditional "who does what around the house" roles have to change a bit, too:

- Husbands, you can't come home and flop into your aptly named "Lazyboy" chair and expect your wife to cook a three-course dinner if she has been working at the office all day.

- Wives, you shouldn't stoically shoulder more than you can handle (all the while building up resentment for the "big loaf" because he won't carry his share of the load).

If both of you are working at jobs, then all the work around the house will have to be a cooperative effort. But this should be the case even if only one of you is bringing home a paycheck. Our society is past the era when only women did the laundry and men could cook only if it involved charcoal and barbeque tongs.

It doesn't really matter who is doing what, so long as both of you are helping to get it done.

. . .In the Small Stuff

- Alternate the chores. It will give you a greater appreciation for what your spouse does.

- When faced with menial tasks around the home, it is better to roll up your sleeves than turn up your nose.

- If a woman's work is never done, it's probably because she asked her husband to help her with some of it.

- You show respect for your spouse when you express appreciation for what he or she does.

- If you need to learn appreciation for your spouse's efforts at home, calculate what it would cost to hire someone to do the same thing.

Time is a very precious gift;
so precious that it's only given
to us moment by moment.

Amelia Barr

THIRTY-SIX

TIME PRESSURE
AND FATIGUE

What would you do if you had all the time in the world? How would you react if you could sleep as long as you wanted, as often as you wanted? You might rejoice and fall on your knees in thanks. You would also pinch yourself to see if you were dreaming.

If you are an average person in a typical marriage with the usual schedule (due to work, family, and other commitments), then your two biggest challenges in life are time pressure and fatigue. Don't just take our word for it. Experts like Dr. James Dobson have been saying it for years. One of the unfortunate by-products of our culture is that people are always strapped for time—and as a result, they are very tired.

Perhaps it's because we are a bunch of overachievers, caught up in the success syndrome. For as long as we can remember, people have been telling us that we can "have it all." Never mind that they were selling beer, cars, travel, clothing, and military service. The messages keep coming—

- You only live once!
- Go for the gusto!
- Be all that you can be!
- The chance of a lifetime!
- Limited time offer!

—until we buy into the fantasy (even if we don't buy all the products).

So the fantasy becomes our driving force, pushing us to achieve more, earn more, buy more, and be more. And the only way we can even get close to realizing our dreams of success is to work harder and do more.

Perhaps we're oversimplifying the problem, but we hope you get the point. Success has a price. There's no free lunch, and only the strong survive. (There go the clichés again.)

Not for a minute are we suggesting that you fail to do your best and shoot for success. We are not endorsing laziness or inactivity. Rising above the level of mediocrity should be your daily goal. But you must go into every job and project, whether you are being paid or not, with your eyes wide open. The Bible calls this "counting the cost." It means estimating in advance how much will be required of you to complete the task. If you can't finish it while keeping your life in balance, don't even start. Otherwise, you are going to run out of time and gas.

Pace yourself. Life is a marathon, not a sprint. Too many of us attack the race like that silly rabbit rather than the wise tortoise, and we end up paying the price. Yes, life takes energy. But it also takes wisdom to know the difference between the costly success and true success.

Time pressure and fatigue can affect your marriage. You may be overcommitted to activities and programs that have nothing to do with work. As we've said before, you can overcommit to some very worthwhile causes, including your church. Before you do, sit down with your spouse and "count the cost." Go in with your eyes open.

Now, before you do anything else, get a good night's sleep!

. . .IN THE SMALL STUFF

- It's easy to say "yes." Saying "no" is what's tough.

- You may not need eight hours of sleep each night, but you need more than you're getting now.

- If you feel there aren't enough hours in the day, you are doing too much.

- Few people do their best work under pressure.

- Don't ever believe that you are the only person capable of doing something right.

- You cannot increase the hours in your day, but you can decrease your commitments.

- As you decrease your commitments to others, increase your commitment to your spouse.

N o man goes before his time—
unless his boss leaves early.

Groucho Marx

THIRTY-SEVEN

WORKING TOGETHER: YOU AREN'T THE BOSS OF ME!

Married couples should spend as much time together as possible. . .as a general rule. But there are some notable circumstances that require an in-depth analysis of your compatibility under stress. Please give serious thought to whether you and your spouse should:

- Hang wallpaper together. This could be danger-
  ous because this activity involves lots of tension

in a confined space, and one of you will have a razor-blade knife.

- Go skydiving together. You want to make sure that you haven't offended your spouse in any way before he or she packs your parachute.

- Take a cross-country car trip. There aren't many radio stations in Wyoming, so you better be good conversationalists or you'll be stuck singing "One Hundred Bottles of Beer on the Wall" as an a cappella duet.

But these activities are just child's play compared to the greatest threat of all to marital harmony: working together.

Most jobs usually have only one boss. What the boss says goes. Those who are subordinate to the boss might be able to express their opinions and offer their suggestions, but in the end, the boss gets what the boss wants. And you better perform up to the level of the boss's expectations, or you can expect to say good-bye soon.

The hierarchy of boss and subordinates may work well in the office, but most marriages don't work that way. So, if you are going to be working with your spouse, you have to be prepared that your relationship in the office may be completely different than your relationship at home. (This is especially true if the office is in the spare bedroom, only fifteen feet away from the bed where you sleep next to your spouse. A little friction in the "office" may lead to some sleepless—and lonely—nights.)

Don't embark into a working relationship without discussing the dynamics first:

- How are decisions going to be made?

- Is there going to be a boss? (And if so, who is it going to be?)

- Are there going to be other workers involved, and how is your married status going to affect them?

- How are you going to handle criticism without it affecting that whole bedroom thing?

If you don't have a clear understanding on these issues from the outset, you'll have problems. Each of you is going to have to give the other a little slack. Life gets difficult when you have to be schizophrenic. ("What time is it? Am I in my spouse role or my office mode?") Be willing to budge a little, and don't get offended easily. Any misunderstanding will produce an unhappy boss or an unhappy employee, and either way there will be an unhappy spouse in your marriage.

. . .IN THE SMALL STUFF

- Consider that your spouse is working with you, not working for you.

- Be willing to concede that your way may not be the best way.

- Paying your spouse a salary doesn't relieve you of the responsibility to pay a compliment.

- If you're working with your spouse, let God be the arbitrator of your employment disputes.

- Make sure you don't ask your spouse to do something that you wouldn't do yourself.

Keep your eyes open before marriage,
half shut afterwards.

Benjamin Franklin

THIRTY-EIGHT

KEEPING YOUR AFFECTIONS
AT HOME
(WHERE THEY BELONG)

If you work outside the home, then you probably spend more time with your friends at work than you do with your family at home. We're not trying to make you feel bad. That's just the way it is.

We're not going to suggest that you change your work schedule to bring it into balance with your home life. You know what you can handle, and only you can truly assess your needs and make the necessary changes. But we are going to offer some advice on keeping your affections at home, where they belong.

Here's what we mean. Because you have a lot in common with your coworkers, friendships develop easily. The longer you know your friends at work, the greater the chances that you'll talk about personal stuff, such as how things are going at home, whether good or bad. If one of your co-workers happens to be attractive, well, let's just say the potential for a problem is there.

You don't want to be a cold fish, but you can do a few things to guard against any kind of inappropriate involvement with someone at work. If you're a man, never under any circumstance meet with a female co-worker behind closed doors or after hours, even if she's your assistant. Never mind that your intentions are completely above board. The rumor mill never is.

If you are a woman, refuse to be drawn into a private meeting with a male co-worker behind closed doors or after hours. You're in a little tougher position than your male counterparts, because that other worker may be your boss, and he may not have the noblest character in the company.

When it comes to your job, the overriding principle comes from Scripture: "Work hard and cheerfully at whatever you do, as though you were working for the Lord rather than for people" (Colossians 3:23).

This advice from Scripture applies to the diligent way you do your job, but it also impacts the kind of person you are around other people. The way you act and everything you say at work should honor the Lord.

Finally, a healthy love life at home is the best insurance policy against taking your affections to work. This verse from Proverbs—written to husbands but equally applicable to wives—summarizes what we mean:

> *Rejoice in the wife of your youth. . . . May you always be captivated by her love.*
> PROVERBS 5:18–19

. . .In the Small Stuff

- The phenomenon of the office romance is well documented. Make sure you don't become one of the statistics.

- Don't tolerate the unwelcome affections and advances of a co-worker or boss. Be friendly but firm in your refusal to get involved.

- Thank God that He has designed marriage to contain your affections.

- Refrain from sharing your personal problems at work.

- Avoid becoming the office "counselor," especially if you're the boss.

- The time to be professional is at work. The time to be affectionate is at home.

- Your coworkers should know that you have a happy marriage.

- Every once in a while, send your spouse a bouquet of flowers at work.

- Avoid criticizing your spouse's job.

- Tell your spouse how much you appreciate the work he or she does to support your family.

- Trust—don't suspect—your spouse.

I want to skip vacation this year
and get a good rest.

Lucille S. Harper

RECREATION

THIRTY-NINE

VACATIONS ARE SUPPOSED TO BE A WASTE OF TIME

Your lives are packed with activities: meetings, appointments, errands, and jobs. Time is too precious to waste. And if you're guilty of carrying that same attitude with you when you go on vacation, then you'll hear yourself saying things like:

- We have to drive 487.3 miles today or we will fall behind schedule.

- We'll have an extra morning for sight-seeing if we take the plane that leaves home at 2 A.M.

- I've made a list of the top fifty attractions. With six days of vacation, that's 8.3 sites per day.

- I don't care that it's DaVinci's *Mona Lisa*, you're only allowed to spend forty-seven seconds per painting so we can leave the museum in time to see the Cheese of the World exhibit.

We agree that there is an educational benefit to visiting all of the state capitals (but we don't think you have to see them all in a single two-week summer vacation). But your vacations with your spouse don't all have to be of historic value; a few of them should be of romantic value. There needs to be time when the two of you can "get away from it all" and just waste time together.

Don't mistakenly think that romantic vacations all require expensive air travel and a view of the Eiffel Tower or barefoot strolls on the sands of Tahiti. You can find romance at the bed-and-breakfast inn a few hours away (and we're not talking about the downtown YMCA). If you wait until you save the $8,000 for a trip to France, you may never get there. A weekend at the lake will benefit your marriage more than a dream vacation to Europe that never happens.

These romantic getaways require that you are committed to relaxing and doing it together:

Husbands: You might want to relax by playing the
championship golf course—but if your wife
doesn't golf, don't be surprised if she wants to
relax by swinging a five iron at your head (or
would a sand wedge be better for cranium
bashing?).
Wives: Even though you enjoy it, your husband is
going to find little delight in an afternoon
spent in the fashion department at Nordstrom's.

Find something you can both do together that will help you

unwind. Whatever it is, it won't be a waste of time if you are with each other.

. . .In the Small Stuff

- The road to romance often requires getting out of town.

- The best time to relax with your spouse is immediately after you've had a vacation with the kids.

- When you're planning to take a vacation with your spouse, agree to travel light: Leave your worries and problems at home.

- A change of scenery will change your outlook.

- If you are tempted to run away when the pressure and stress get too great, just do it (but take your spouse with you).

Whenever I get the urge to exercise,
I sit down until the urge passes.

Somebody famous
(but we can't remember who)

FORTY

EXERCISE. . .
EVEN IF IT KILLS YOU

People seem to be dieting a lot these days. There's the Atkins diet, the Weigh Down diet, the Low Fat diet, and the Sugar Busters diet. There's Weight Watchers, Jenny Craig, and The Schwarzbein Principle. Without a doubt, we know how to lose weight. What we struggle with is keeping it off.

Should we even worry about losing weight? We probably do not need to worry to the degree that the diet marketers are telling us, but there are compelling health reasons for all of us to stay fit. The thing is, weight loss is only part of the story. The other part is exercise. Actually, the two go together like love and marriage. Health guru Stormie Omartian says, "Exercise is just as important in weight loss as proper diet."

The great thing about exercise is that it can be fun. You really can't say that about dieting, because denying yourself is never fun. Conversely, exercise is all about adding variety to your life—walking, jogging, biking, hiking, tennis, and yes, even golf.

If exercise has never been a part of your routine, do yourself a favor and start. And if you can, exercise with your spouse. You will enjoy it. Instead of envying those couples in your neighborhood who walk together, be one of them! More and more we've been hearing about couples who golf together. Terrific! Go for it. Buy some clubs, take some lessons, and walk the fairways together. We also just met a couple who rides a tandem bicycle. How romantic is that?

Don't feel like you have to spend a lot of money on exercise. Just start walking together. It might become the best part of your day.

...IN THE SMALL STUFF

- Exercise is all about health, not competition.

- You can use equipment to exercise, but it's not necessary.

- You can join a health club to exercise, but you don't have to.

- Exercise outside as much as you can.

- When you exercise with your spouse, try to stay at the same pace.

The only exercise some people get
is jumping to conclusions,
running down their friends,
sidestepping responsibility,
dodging issues, passing the buck,
and pushing their luck.

Anonymous

FORTY-ONE

YOU CAN'T AFFORD
ANOTHER FAD

Because our lives are so hectic, we are always on the lookout for the newest idea or device that will simplify our life. Our schedule is out of control, so we'll grasp at any fad or trend that promises to bring balance, convenience, or time to our schedules. If you want to deny this obvious fact, we suggest you look around the house and spot the decaying carcasses of exercise gadgets that were long-ago abandoned. For instance:

- The television cabinet contains an exercise video that was going to give us buns of steel (or titanium, or pewter, just anything except the buns of porridge that we're packing now).

- In the bedroom is a metal contraption that looks like a medieval torture device. It uses a bicycle movement for your legs while your arms go in a helicopter motion. Now it stands idle, like a bedside valet, and it will be used for hanging a bathrobe and either brassieres or neckties (depending on whose side of the bed is closest to it).

- And let's not overlook the Flab-Eliminator on the shelf in the hall closet. In case you blocked the horrifying episode from your memory, it had the electrodes that you stuck to your abdomen with duct tape so pulsating current would constrict your stomach muscles while you slept so you would never have to get up to exercise. After two weeks, the only effect was a spastic bowel, so you got plenty of exercise getting up several times each night.

But we aren't attracted to shortcuts only when it comes to exercise. If we can find them, we'll take any crazy seminar if it promises to solve the problems in our marriage. So, one weekend you might be sitting in a lotus position on the floor next to your spouse with John Tesh music playing in the background and the scent of Herbal Tranquillity potpourri in the air. The next month you might be spending a day at the Aggression Release Clinic as you and your spouse role-play as archenemy WWF wrestlers.

Sometimes we even think we can get a "quick fix" in our spiritual lives:

- Wives enroll their husbands in the church's "Manly Men's Conference" to get them spiritually supercharged. (This year's theme: "Drop-Kick Me, Jesus, Through the Goal Posts of Life.")

- Wives go to the women's retreat. (This is a lot like the men's conference, but with tablecloths, doilies, and table centerpieces—and without the belching and other bodily emissions.)

Shortcuts and quick fixes don't work when it comes to the physical, marital, and spiritual dimensions of your life. The devices and programs you have tried can be effective (with the notable exception of the Flab-Eliminator), but there will be no long-lasting change in your life if you go back to your old habits of being overcommitted, overworked, and overtired.

You are going to regain balance in your life only as you learn to discipline yourself to include relaxation and quietness as a part of your schedule. You need to spend some "quiet time" with God; you and your spouse need to capture a few moments together; and you even need some time being alone with your own thoughts. If you haven't done much of this before, then it will be difficult at first, but you will notice the benefits right away.

If your life needs to calm down a little, you won't find

the answer on the home shopping channel or on any infomercial. You know what you have to do. Now just make it a priority.

. . .IN THE SMALL STUFF

- You have to step off the merry-go-round if you want your life to stop spinning.

- A little bit of rest every day is better than a lot once a year.

- When you are too busy to spare any time for relaxation is precisely when you need it.

- Don't get wound so tight that you can't unwind at the end of the day.

- Overcommitment is not a virtue.

I have never counseled a dying man
who regretted not having made more money,
but quite a few regretted not having
spent enough time with their families.

Charles Swindoll

FORTY-TWO

THE BEST THINGS
IN LIFE ARE FREE

In our consumer society, we have a tendency to think that the best things in life come from the pages of *Architectural Digest*, the *Robb Report*, or *Travel & Leisure*. Well, if you think that the best things in life are things—and nice things at that—you may have a problem.

But we suspect you don't really think things make you happy, at least not after the newness wears off. It's the stuff you can't buy—even if you had all the money in the world—

that really brings joy to your life.

These are your relationships, your experiences, and your dreams. You know what they are. You've known about them for years, and yet you keep overlooking them. To help remind you, here's a little list we have compiled just to get you thinking. Feel free to add your own "Best Things in Life."

. . .IN THE SMALL STUFF

- Walking along the ocean shore in the fog.

- Finishing a great book.

- Waking up next to your spouse and realizing that you don't have to do anything or be any-where—at least not today.

- Feeling the little arms of your young child wrapped tightly around your neck.

- Getting a back rub from your spouse.

- Hearing your teenagers talk about their day.

- Listening to your favorite romantic CD with the lights turned low.

- Snuggling in front of the perfect fire.

- Having your family gathered around the table at Thanksgiving.

- Watching *It's a Wonderful Life* for the fortieth time.

- Decorating your Christmas tree together.

- Kissing your spouse on New Year's Eve and looking forward to another year together.

- Growing old together.

Whenever men gather,
they soon turn the conversation to
the subject of women
and in the opinions that are given
reveal themselves as divided into two categories—
the men who would rather run away from women
and the men who would rather run away with them.

Carl Riblet, Jr.

FOR WIVES ONLY

FORTY-THREE

THE MALE EGO: HANDLE WITH CARE

Wives, this chapter is for you alone. Don't let your husband read it, or he'll know that you have discovered his weakness.

You've got to think of your husband like a Tootsie Roll Pop. We don't mean to say that he is a sucker. Nor are we trying to imply that he is most useful if you poke him with a little stick. We're just trying to give you a metaphor for his psyche: When you get through his tough, hard shell, then he can be soft and sweet on the inside.

You might prefer that the soft and sweet part of your husband was a little more accessible, but that's not how men are. Their egos demand that they be viewed by you, and members of their own species, as tough, virile, testosterone factories. When you ask your husband if he is in touch with his feminine side, he'll deny having one—and he'll be repulsed at the thought of touching it.

We must give you a word of caution: Although your husband has this outside shell of bravado, it is quite fragile. Sure, he is a legend in his own mind, but he needs to hear that you think he is great. This probably goes back to the Garden of Eden days when Adam needed to hear Eve say:

You killed a big saber-toothed mammoth. You're my hero. You are the bravest and strongest man on earth.

Of course, Eve could say this truthfully because at the time Adam was the only man on earth. You'll have to be a bit more creative because now a lot of other men are around, and hopefully the only thing your husband is likely to kill is a mosquito. You're going to have to convince him that you find other qualities just as manly—for instance, his sense of responsibility, his ability to keep his promises, his courage to be vulnerable, his gentle strength.

If you want to get to his soft and sweet center, you'll have to show your husband that you are impressed with his strong outer shell.

. . .IN THE SMALL STUFF

- Your husband is not tough as he wants you to think he is.

- Testosterone must affect memory. It appears to impede recollection of birth dates and anniversaries, but it enhances retention of sports statistics.

- If your husband were the last man on earth, you would still have to tell him that he is the best.

Any man who says he can
read a woman like a book
is probably illiterate.

Anonymous

FORTY-FOUR

THE DREADED "S" WORD

(AND WE DON'T MEAN "SEX")

Wives, this chapter is also written for you, but we give you permission to let your husbands read it. Both of you need to have a clear understanding of the infamous "S" word. It is a word so controversial we are afraid to speak of it. Oh, well, here goes: submission. There, we said it. It is a word that has politicized marriage in a society that intends for women to have opportunities equal to men.

Now, before you bristle at the thought of reading what

two married men have to say about wifely submission, let us remind you that we each have an unmarried adult daughter. We would not want our daughters living a subservient existence under the tyrannical rule of some dolt of a husband. (Does that make you feel a little better?)

If you are opposed to the concept of submission in marriage, don't complain to us about it. Take it up with God because God designed marriage that way. And don't be so defensive. Actually, God's plan for marriage is that both spouses should be deferential and respectful to each other. Look at what the Apostle Paul wrote about marriage:

> *You will submit to one another out of reverence for Christ. . . . You wives will submit to your husbands as you do to the Lord. . . . And you husbands must love your wives with the same love Christ showed the Church.*
>
> EPHESIANS 5:21–22, 25

With that Scripture as a framework, let's think about how submission works when you move it off the pages of the Bible and into the family room:

- The role of submission is reciprocal. Wives are to be submissive to their husbands, but the husbands are to be Christlike—and Christ's love meant that He surrendered His entire being for our good. Because Christ set a pattern of love, respect, and supreme self-sacrifice, the husband should be approaching his role with the attitude of a servant, not a dictator.

- Submission doesn't require that you forfeit your opinions. Both husband and wife should be participating fully in the family decisions. God gave you both brains and personalities, and He doesn't intend for either of you to disconnect them when a wedding ring is slipped on your finger.

- Wives, don't wait to be submissive until your husband becomes the perfect Christlike servant leader. "I'll do it only when he does it" is not submission; it is stubbornness. If need be, you start (and maybe your attitude will prompt change in your husband).

Our culture mocks the concept of a woman who is submissive. On the other hand, God exalts a woman in that role. Throughout history, it seems that God's wisdom has proven to be much more reliable than the trends of society. Buck the trend.

. . .IN THE SMALL STUFF

- It will be easier for your husband to show love to you if you respond lovingly toward him.

- Don't think of submission as a concession to your husband; think of it as an act of worship to God and a gift to your marriage.

- Your husband married you to be his wife, not his mother. If he wanted to be bossed, nagged, and lectured, he would still be living in his parents' house.

- Most husbands are reluctant to ask for directions. A submissive wife won't yell at him for getting lost, but she'll offer him the map she put in her purse before they left home.

Men derive their sacred value
from being trusted and admired,
women derive theirs from being cared for.

David Riddell

FORTY-FIVE

THE OTHER DREADED
"S" WORD
(THIS TIME WE DO
MEAN WHAT YOU THINK)

Why is it that husbands and wives have such different attitudes toward sex? This question has puzzled married couples since creation. In this chapter, we'll try to answer that question, from a male perspective.

Keep in mind that we are not experts in this field (no man is). Our only qualifications are that we've been married to the same wives for more than twenty-five years, which means we have more than fifty years of experience between us. That's fifty years of trying to figure out how to get our wives to have more sex. With us.

Men view sex as one of the best things around—and one of life's necessities as well. Unfortunately, some men have extrapolated this viewpoint a little further: They think that sex is their God-given right. This view has led to all sorts of problems, because when you think you have a right to something, you tend to take it. And we know God never intended for men to take sex, yet that's exactly what some of us try to do.

What God does intend is for sex to be something shared between a man and a woman. It's a reciprocal activity, designed to give both partners great joy. But not just any man and woman can be sex partners; God is very clear that sex has to be confined to the boundaries of marriage. C. S. Lewis called sex outside of marriage a "monstrosity," because in God's view, marriage is a total union that makes a man and woman "one flesh." When a man or woman has sex outside of marriage in any way or at any time, it's like tearing your flesh apart (not a pretty picture).

As men, we need to understand that sex is God's gift to

us. And since it's a gift, sex is a privilege, not a right. Sex is about partners demonstrating their love with their bodies—and giving each other pleasure in the process. So if you are each expressing love and seeking to give pleasure, then neither of you will look at sex as something you take from the other.

. . .IN THE SMALL STUFF

- If a man is fully joined to his wife, he needs to leave his father and mother (Genesis 2:24).

- Sex is God's wedding gift to the bride and groom.

- Guard what you say in the bedroom. Your husband takes your words very seriously.

- Tell your husband how much you enjoy him.

Your marriage is in trouble if your wife says,
"You're only interested in one thing,"
and you can't remember what it is.

Milton Berle

FOR HUSBANDS ONLY

FORTY-SIX

WHERE
SEX BEGINS

We have talked to wives about sex from a husband's point of view; now it's time to talk about sex from a wife's perspective. Unfortunately, we aren't as qualified in this area, so we decided to consult with a couple of experts: our wives. After conducting a series of tests—including lengthy questionnaires, personal one-on-one interviews, and blind studies—we have come up with some very useful information for husbands everywhere. (Actually, we didn't do any of that. We just asked our wives and they told us what to say.)

Guys, let's face it, women are very different from us, especially in the area of sex. In their view, sex is not the "end all and be all" of marriage. (Yes, it shocked us, too.) Whereas we see sex as a piece of cake, to them sex is the icing on the cake.

Here's another update. If you and your wife don't have good communication before, during, and after sex (which is basically all of the time), then sex becomes an act rather than communion. (Just so you know, two people have communion when they exchange thoughts and feelings and have a close spiritual relationship.) The bottom line is this: A married couple should achieve true intimacy with good sex and great communication.

Whoa, this is getting deep. And there's more. For a woman, sex is part of the whole package of love that includes talking, listening, and nonsexual touching—all of the small stuff of your marriage—that goes on all the time. In other words, sex is a process. It's not that our wives don't need or want sex. They just want it in the context of true love. We've got a feeling that's the way God wants it, too.

That's about it, men. This may not be everything, but there is plenty here for all of us to work on.

. . .In the Small Stuff

- Sex is a privilege, not a right.

- Don't base your entire marriage on the quality of your sex life.

- Sex is more than a physical act.

- Sex is a gift a husband and wife give each other.

- Tell your wife how much you enjoy her.

Don't deny your dominant temperament,
but do temper your natural tendencies.

Gary Smalley

FORTY-SEVEN

AVERT YOUR GLANCE

This is another "husbands only" chapter. And, guys, if you didn't read the last chapter ("Where Sex Begins"), read it now. You need to be reminded that sex tends to be a biological urge for husbands, but for wives it is an important part of the whole romance and love process. This is a fundamental concept for understanding this chapter.

Women are not immune to noticing an attractive

man. We are told that many women give a second glance if they like the way a guy looks in his Levi's. (We had to get this information secondhand because we have no personal experience with this phenomenon.) But women are rookies when it comes to "checking out" the opposite sex.

Admit it. As guys, checking out members of the opposite sex was our cultural experience since before we had facial hair. Studies have shown that soon after the onset of puberty, the most often-repeated phrase in a man's vocabulary is "Check out that babe." Hopefully, that changes with maturity.

Once you become a husband, your vows of love, loyalty, and honor to your wife require that your sexual impulses (what you do and think) should be reserved for her alone. Unfortunately, your physiological proclivity for appreciation of the female framework and the spectrum of its diversity won't evaporate as you walk down the wedding chapel aisle with your bride.

Some men seem to think that they are incapable of keeping their sexual attentions focused on their wives. But they can. Successful husbands make a conscientious effort to intentionally look away from any view that would stimulate improper. . .you know. . .urges.

We don't mean that you have to walk down the street with your eyes closed, but your sexual loyalty to your wife will be protected if:

- You resist the urge to lean over your secretary's shoulder whenever she wears that blue V-neck sweater.

- You choose restaurants based on the quality of the cuisine, not the outfits of the waitresses.

- You don't surf the Internet through any site that uses "hot" or "wild" or the slang name of any female body part in its .com address.

- You throw away the Victoria's Secret catalog as soon as it arrives (and we won't accept your excuse that you only read the articles, because it doesn't have any articles).

When a man cheats on his wife, it doesn't begin in a motel room. He starts cheating on her the moment he starts looking at and thinking about another woman. Stay loyal to your wife by looking at her alone. You'll be amazed at how sexually appealing your wife is if she's the only woman you ever look at with sex in mind.

. . .IN THE SMALL STUFF

- "Look All You Want but Don't Touch" is a great rule for museums, but it is not the philosophy that a married man should have toward other women. Too much looking can lead to touching.

- You won't fall off a cliff if you make sure you stay away from the edge.

- You can fantasize about any woman you want,

so long as in real life she is wearing your wedding ring.

- Always give your wife the impression that in your eyes she is the most gorgeous woman in the world.

- Keep your eyes where they belong: in your head and on your wife.

- There is a lot of meaning behind the words, "I do." Part of that promise means you "do" with your wife and you "won't" with other women.

Love is patient and kind.
Love is not jealous or boastful or proud or rude.
Love does not demand its own way.
Love is not irritable,
and it keeps no record of
when it has been wronged.

1 Corinthians 13:4–5

FORTY-EIGHT

THE TRUE MEANING
OF LOVE

Love is not something you do. It's more an expression of who you are. This principle is clearly illustrated by God Himself, who is the epitome of love. In fact, that's what the Bible says: "God is love" (1 John 4:8). God ultimately defines love because love fills every part of His being. Since God is infinite and eternal, so is His love.

The amazing thing is that this infinite God of love has decided to focus His love on us, His created beings. Because

God made us in His image (Genesis 1:26), He knows us ultimately and intimately. Nobody knows us better than God does, and His greatest desire is that we know Him in return.

There's only one problem. God is perfect and we're not. A perfect being cannot have communion—that is, exchange thoughts and feelings and have a close spiritual relationship—with imperfect beings. That's why God decided to send His only Son, Jesus Christ, into the world to die for our imperfections (in other words, our sin).

God didn't wait for us to love Him on our own. He sent Jesus to die for us while we were still sinners (Romans 5:8). All we have to do is believe that what God did for us is true and effective, the only way for us to have communion with Him forever (John 3:16).

Deep down in our souls we long for what God wants to give us: complete intimacy. Intimacy is the key ingredient of love and very much a part of love's true meaning. We are incapable of that kind of love on our own, but with God's help we can both give and receive this true love.

God has designed marriage as the container for true love. Don't let anyone tell you otherwise. Because marriage is ordained by God, it is His sacred gift to us. Marriage is the place where a man and a woman can truly know and truly love each other with every dimension and fiber of their beings— emotionally, physically, mentally, and spiritually.

True love isn't easy, and it doesn't happen by itself. It takes two people trusting God as they work toward the same goal: intimacy.

. . .IN THE SMALL STUFF

- There is no way to find true love apart from God.

- True love is found in a Person.

- God loves you even if you don't love Him.

- You have a very compelling reason to love God: He loved you first.

- The world doesn't need love. The world needs to love.

T rust us:
One day your kids will
grow up and leave home.
That's why it's so important to find
mutual enjoyment in
each other's interests and hobbies now.

Dave and Claudia Arp

GROWING OLDER TOGETHER

FORTY-NINE

REDECORATE YOUR LIVES

When your kids leave home, you'll be tempted to redecorate the house. But the house isn't the only thing that needs some redecorating attention. So does your marriage. When you have kids at home, they consume the time, resources, and attention of your marriage. When they leave home, you're likely to have time and money to spare (which is a situation you haven't seen since before you had kids).

Think of the possibilities for rejuvenating your marriage after the kids have left home:

- Any night can be "date night" for the two of you. You don't have to worry about the car being gone when you want to use it.

- A quiet evening together watching the logs burn in the fireplace is not going to be interrupted by a bunch of teenagers tromping through the house to graze in the refrigerator.

- You can doze off watching television in the family room without fear that your kids will sabotage you by sticking chocolate raisins up your nostrils while you sleep.

- You can be amorous in the living room.

Life with "just the two of you" doesn't have to be gloomy. It can be fantastic. All you need to do is discover the possibilities.

...In the Small Stuff

- The arrival of a child in a marriage is a blessed event. After about twenty years, so is the child's departure.

- When your kids leave home, you can resume doing what created them in the first place.

- After your children move out of the house, some of the rooms will be empty, but your lives don't have to be.

- Kids brighten up a house, but that's because they never turn off the lights.

- With the kids away, you can afford to go out for dinner at a place with linen napkins.

J ust about the time parents think
their job is done,
they become grandparents.

Anonymous

FIFTY

NOW YOUR NEST IS EMPTY—
NOW IT'S NOT!

That day you've been dreaming about has finally arrived. All of your kids are out of the nest and on their own. You are secure in the knowledge that they are doing well, working toward various goals, serving the Lord wherever they are, promising to settle down and start families someday.

You love it when they come home to visit. You pamper them and attend to their every need, as you would any special guest. When they leave, you're sorry to see them go, but you love it that you and your spouse have the privilege of living this part of your life with complete freedom. You feel like kids again.

Then it happens. Nobody has prepared for it. Your kids didn't plan it, and it certainly wasn't your idea. But it happens. One of your kids moves back home. Maybe your son finished school and he has no prospects—or worse, no ambition. Perhaps your daughter made some poor choices, and now she can't raise her child—your grandchild—alone. Finances could be what caused your child's problem—and after all, you have always been a good provider.

So what do you do? First, you never stop loving your kids; you never stop being a parent. But even though your love doesn't change, your role as a parent does. You can't treat your adult kids the same way you treated your kid kids.

If you have done the best you can to help your kids build an inner scaffolding, then you have to let go and let them experience life on their own. This probably won't come at a single moment, like graduation. It will be more like a process. It's up to you, however, to make sure the process doesn't drag out. Otherwise it's going to drag you down, and you may start resenting your kids.

From the time they are very young, your kids need to know that they will always have a place in your hearts and home. Assure them that there's nothing they can do to make you stop loving them. At the same time, they need to know that the process of leaving home is natural and good—for them and for you. That way, if they ever do return, it's to stay for a while, not forever.

Just as you have ground rules for your children when they are children in your home, you need ground rules for the adult children in your home. The first ground rule should be that this return is temporary. Help your boomerang kids set goals for their recovery and their future, but don't do their work for them. You may have helped with a science fair project more than you should have when they were in grade school, but there's a lot more at stake here than blue ribbons.

Keep your expectations out in the open. Talk together as adults and work toward a solution. The sooner your kids stand on their own, the better it will be for them and for you. If they are going to depend on anyone, your kids should depend on God. He's the most qualified to guide them today, tomorrow, and forever.

. . .IN THE SMALL STUFF

- Your children are God's gift to you, but at some point you have to be willing to give them back to God.

- Always have a place for your kids to stay when they come home.

- When they leave, tell your kids that you're proud of them for making it on their own.

- You don't have to cut the financial strings when your kids move out, but eventually they should be cut (the strings, not the kids).

- You can't buy your kids' love.

- Helping your kids find work is fine, but don't do the work for them.

- You are more valuable to your kids as a career counselor than you are as an employment agency.

- Hiring your kids to work in the family business can be a wonderful experience, but it can also lead to resentment and heartache.

- If you hire your kids, show them respect rather than privilege.

- Always remember that your spouse is your first love, not your kids.

My parents stayed together for forty years,
but that was out of spite.

Woody Allen

FIFTY-ONE

DON'T LET YOUR GOLDEN YEARS TURN BROWN

Routines and predictability can be nice, but after a while they can lead to boredom. And boredom sours marriage faster than a bowl of guacamole spoils in the noonday sun.

The later years of your marriage don't have to be a downward spiral for your mental functions and physical pursuits. Your golden years may give you the freedom to enjoy opportunities that were previously unavailable to you.

- You can go to new places. If you are no longer tied down to a job, you'll have the freedom to travel. Both of you should be involved in planning the trips, so you'll both enjoy the destination.

- You can learn new things. Don't let new technology isolate you from the rest of society. Keep up with innovations. (This will give you something to talk about with your grandchildren.)

- You can meet new people. Don't feel compelled to spend all of your socializing with people your own age. Your enduring marriage is a great example for younger couples (because most marriages don't make it to a double-digit anniversary).

Your marriage will never become boring or routine if both you and your spouse keep improving yourselves.

. . .IN THE SMALL STUFF

- You aren't getting older if you keep getting better.

- The best things in life may be free, but the senior's discount helps with the rest.

- Don't let your spouse's mind go to waste.

- Your next place to go should be someplace you've never been.

- You've got a lot of good friends out there you haven't met yet.

The development of
a really good marriage
is not a natural process.
It's an achievement.

David and Vera Mace

FIFTY-TWO

YOUR MARRIAGE IS
YOUR GREATEST LEGACY

There's a huge misconception out there about marriage. Many people think that they are the ones responsible for making their marriages work. They have come to believe that somehow in our cleverness, we humans came up with the idea of marriage in the first place. Consequently, the individuals involved are more important than the marriage.

Our society has reduced marriage to a legal contract. In

some places all you have to do to get married is make a small payment. This is what happens when we imperfect mortals take something sacred—like marriage—and bring it down to our level. We goof it up! The proof is found in the fact that nearly half of all marriages end in divorce. To avoid this nasty prospect, many couples ignore marriage altogether and simply live together.

If you're married or considering marriage, you need to understand that marriage is more than a contract. Marriage is God's beautiful gift to you and your spouse. It is His idea for you to grow together for life as you both grow in Him. In that respect marriage can be and should be your greatest legacy.

A legacy is something of value you leave to those who follow you. If your marriage is characterized by true love, integrity, and selflessness, then you are telling those around you—especially your children—that marriage is God's idea and not yours. You are saying that your commitment to each other is based on God's standard, not the world's.

As a legacy, your marriage is much bigger than the two of you. It is a representation of God Himself. You see, for people who see God as a formal ritual or an impersonal force, your marriage may be the clearest picture of God's true love they ever see.

. . .IN THE SMALL STUFF

- Take marriage seriously. God does.

- Have fun in your marriage.

- Just because you have trouble doesn't mean your marriage isn't working.

- Rejoice when God brings you through a difficult time.

- Your marriage is a greater testimony of God's love and grace than your words.

- The legacy of your marriage will live for generations.

ALL ABOUT BRUCE & STAN

Bruce Bickel is a lawyer, and **Stan Jantz** is a retail-marketing consultant. But that's not what they really like to do best. Bruce and Stan spend their free time as "cultural commentators" (they made up that term), observing how God applies to everyday life. Together they have written fifteen books, and they host a weekly radio program, *The Bruce & Stan Show*.

Bruce and Stan are certainly qualified to write this book. They have been married for more than fifty years (but not to each other). Bruce and Cheryl have been married for twenty-five years in a row and have two grown children, Lindsey and Matt. With uncanny symmetry, Stan has been married to Karin for twenty-five years in a row, and they have two grown children, Hillary and Scott.

Other books by the authors include:
God Is in the Small Stuff (and it all matters)
God Is in the Small Stuff for Your Family

Bruce & Stan's Guide to God
Bruce & Stan's Guide to the Bible
Bruce & Stan's Guide to the End of the World
Onyourown.com-email messages to my daughter

Bruce and Stan would enjoy hearing from you. You may write words of effusive praise, hearty encouragement, or gentle criticism to them at:

Email:guide@bruceandstan.com

Send Mail to:

Bruce & Stan,
P.O. Box 25565, Fresno CA 93729–5565

You can learn more than you want to know about Bruce and Stan by visiting their website:

www.bruceandstan.com

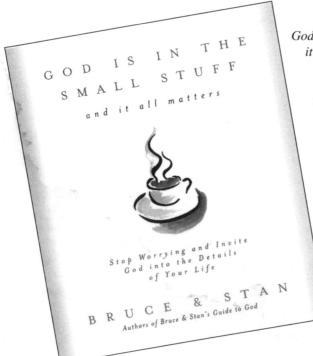